TAXATION: APPLICATION AND ITS DEVELOPMENT IN SOUTH SUDAN

Anei Mangong Anei Ngong (BSc., M.A., Ph. D.)

Assistant Professor,

Department of Business Administration

College of Economics and Social Studies

University of Bahr El Ghazal

A Note from the Publisher

The publisher wishes to acknowledge and thank Dr Douglas H. Johnson for his invaluable help and support for Africa World Books and its mission of preserving and promoting African cultural and literary traditions and history. Dr Johnson and fellow historians have been instrumental in ensuring that African people remain connected to their past and their identity. Africa World Books is proud to carry on this mission.

© *Anei Mangong Anei*, 2021

ISBN: 978-0-6453633-9-5
978-0-6453633-8-8 (Hardcover)

Cover design, typesetting and layout : Africa World Books

Africa
World Books
Pty Ltd

Dedication

To my dear parents, wives, and children

Contents

Tables And Figures:

Preface

Taxation as a course for Third Year, Department of Business Administration, University of Bahr El Ghazal, lacked reference books at the time the Department of Business Administration started to admit students for specialization in 2008. This compelled the author to make a collection from many different sources including interviews with some personnel from the Directorate of Taxation, Ministry of Finance and Planning of the Republic of South Sudan.

The book covers the contents of the course outline of Taxation for Third Year Business Administration option, as well as for those of Post Graduate Diploma in Public Finance.

Taxation is part of public finance of which it was necessary to cover essential issues interrelated with taxation which are integral parts of public finance.

The edition made use of the latest available original documents which contain recent data and information on taxation in the Republic of South Sudan. It covers types of taxes in South Sudan and the budgets from 2011 up to 2017/18 fiscal years.

Much great care was observed to ensure the accuracy in preparation of this book. But if anyone feels that there are errors due to misprint or otherwise, they are welcomed for constructive suggestions for improvement of the book. I'm confident and hopeful that lecturers and students will find this book to be a useful aid to them for the better understanding of the concept and principles of taxation as a course.

I'm indebted to Mr. Albino Chol Thiik, Director General, Directorate of Taxation, Ministry of Finance and Planning, who gave directives to the personnel of the Directorate of Taxation to avail the information I needed.

Moreover, I owe thanks to Mr. Manyok Kuol Jok, Head of Taxation Office and late John Josepk Ucin, Assistant Director for Large Taxpayers Unit, as well as Mr. Joseph Kenyi of Revenue Department, Ministry of Finance and Planning; all who provided the data I needed about taxation of the republic of South Sudan.

Above all, I'm indebted to Mr. Mabior Deu, Director General, Department of Foreign Aid, Ministry of Finance and Planning; and Dr. Olympio Attipio, former Commissioner General, National Revenue Authority; both of them provided information that I required about their units.

Acronyms

ATAF African Tax Administration Forum
BC Before Christ
BIS Bank for International Settlements
BOP Balance of Payments
CDI Commitment to Development Index
DTIS Directorate of Taxation Information System
EU European Community
FY Fiscal Year
GDP Gross Domestic Product
GoSS Government of Southern Sudan
GRSS Government of the Republic of South Sudan
GST Goods and Services Tax
HNWIs High Net Worth Individuals
IDA International Development Agency
IMF International Monetary Fund
IOU I Owe You
LDCs Less developed Countries
LTU Large Taxpayers Unit

MNCs Multinational Corporations
MOUs Memorandum of Understandings
NATO North Atlantic Treaty Organization
NBP National Budget Plan
NFL National Football League
NGOs Non Governmental Organizations
NRA National Revenue Authority
OECD Organization for Economic Cooperation and Development
PAYE Pay As You Earn
SDRs Special Drawing Rights
SMTU Small and Medium Taxpayers Unit
SPLA Sudan Peoples' Liberation Army
SSDP South Sudan Development Plan
UN United Nations
VAT Value Added Tax
WTO World Trade Organization

Chapter One

TAXATION

1.1 Introduction

Taxation is an invariable attribute of an organized political society, and, it is the principal means of raising revenue for public
purposes. Taxation is correlative to the services which government performs for the community. Taxation includes the processes of levying, collecting, and paying taxes. The basis of taxation is wealth and the classification of taxes depends on wealth.

However, "taxation is part of public finance and public finance
is that department of economic theory in which we deal with
the public expenditure and revenue. The importance of public
finance has increased in recent years. These days, the government
is considered responsible to stabilize the economic situation of
the country. Similarly, the government plays important role in

the economic development process. Various measures are taken by the government to increase the rate of economic growth."[1] Different countries have different tax systems and tax structures. They impose different taxes and charge them at different rates. The structure of taxation in a country changes from time to time. The changes are made to reflect the income needs of government, the nature and structure of the economy, population, economic objectives etc. Because of such changes, it is hard to describe a tax structure that is true for a long time.

1.2 Concept and Meaning of Taxation

In Africa, "'Taxation' generally means personal income taxes, corporate taxes, value-added taxes and custom duties. These taxes bring in most national revenue, and –probably for that reason-dominate international discussion of taxation. However, to people outside the big cities and small elite circles, 'taxation' means something very different: smaller taxes, levies and fees paid to local governments; 'informal' payments to tax collectors and state officials; and a wide range of payments to groups other than the government, including traditional chiefs. These kinds of payments are easily overlooked by outsiders but are integral part of the story in Africa."[2]

Worldwide, there are a number of definitions of taxation but some of them are here below:

1. Taxation is the process of assessing, collecting and administering taxes.

---

1   Saleemi, N. A. Taxation I Simplified (Revised Edition). Saleemi Publications Ltd., Nairobi, Kenya, 2007. p. 1.

2   Mick Moore, Wilson Prichard and Odd-Helge F. Jeldstad. Taxing Africa: Coercion, Reform and Development, Zed Books Ltd., London, UK, 2018. P. 2.

2. Taxation is money that has to be paid as taxes. It is the system of collecting money by taxes.

3. Taxation refers to the practice of government collecting money from its citizens to pay for public services.

4. Taxation refers to compulsory or coercive money collections by a levying authority, usually a government. The term "taxation" applies to all types of involuntary levies, from income to capital gains to estate taxes.

5. Taxation is the system by which a government takes money from people and spends it on things such as education, health and defense.

6. Taxation is the process whereby charges are imposed on individuals or property by the legislative branch of the federal government and by many state governments to raise funds for public purposes.

7. Taxation involves extracting resources from taxpayers with no guarantee of any kind of corresponding benefit.[3]

8. Taxation is the sum of money levied according to the law without any service or direct benefit in return for that. It is paid to the government to meet all its public commitments and responsibilities towards the society and for the achievement of its financial, economic and social objectives.[4]

1.3 Historical Background of Taxation

The first known system of taxation was in Ancient Egypt around 3000-2800BC in the first Dynasty of Egypt of the Old Kingdom

---

3   Mick Moore, Wilson Prichard and Odd-Helge F. Jeldstad. Op. cit. p. 11.

4   The Taxation Chamber. Taxation Guide, Khartoum University Press, Khartoum, Sudan, November, 2003. P. 2.

of Egypt.[5]

The earliest and most widespread form of taxation was the Corvée and Tithe. The Corvée was forced labour provided to the State by peasants too poor to pay other forms of taxation (labour in Ancient Egypt is a synonym for taxes).[6] There were other records that Pharaoh collect Tithes from the people. Other records are granary receipts on limestone flakes and papyrus.[7]

Early taxation is also described in the Bible. In Genesis Chapter 47, verse 24-the New International Version, it states "But when the crop comes in, give a fifth of it to Pharaoh." Joseph in Egypt made people to divide their crop, providing a portion to the Pharaoh. A share of 20% of the crop was a special tax gathered against an expected famine.[8]

In the Persian Empire, a regulated and sustainable tax system was introduced by Darius I the Great in 500BC.[9] The Persian system of taxation was tailored to each Satrapy (an area ruled by a provincial governor). The taxes collected were in form of money, silver talents and food for the army. The tax in the Persian Empire was exclusively levied on Satrapies (provinces) based on their lands, productive capacity and tribute levels.[10]

---

5   Taxes in the Ancient World, University of Pennsylvania Almanac, Vol. 48, No. 28, 2 April, 2002.

6   David F. Burg (2004). A World History of Tax Rebellions, Taylor and Francis. Pp. vi-viii.

7   "The Bible".

8   "Darius I (Darius the Great), King of Persia (from 521 BC)". 1902encyclopedia.com.net.Retrieved22January2013.

9   History of Iran (Persia)". Historyworld.net.Retrieved22January2013.

10   British Museum. "History of the World in 100 Objects: Rosetta Stone." BBC.

The Rosetta stone, a tax concession issued by Ptolemy V in 196 BC led to the most decipherment (success) in history - the cracking of hieroglyphics[11] (pictures or symbols of an object that represents a word, syllable or sound used in ancient Egypt and other writing systems).

In Jerusalem Bible, Jesus at the time of Herod, when the Pharisees and some Herodians wanted to catch him–he said that "Pay Caesar what belongs to Caesar–and God what belongs to God" (Mk. 2: 13-17, Mt. 22: 15-21, and Lk. 20: 27-28). In the Gospel of St. Mathew, Jesus at different times found Mathew and Levi sitting at the tax offices and he told them to follow him (Mt. 9:9, Mt.2: 13-14 and Lk. 5: 27-28). "Shekel was paid by Jesus as tax" (Mt. 17: 24-27).

There are numerous records of government tax collection in Europe since at least the 17th Century e.g. France, Netherlands, Scandinavia, England (Britain), and Denmark. Taxation was inform of percentage of production of final goods and may reach 15-20% during that time in France, the Netherlands and Scandinavia. During the war-filled years of the 18th and early 19th centuries, tax rates in Europe increased dramatically as war became more expensive and governments became more centralized and adept (good or skillful) at gathering taxes. This increase was greatest in England, the burden increased by 85% over this period. In France, taxes were lower but the burden was mainly on landowners, individuals and internal trade and thus created far more resentment. However, the taxes of today are different from those of former times.[12]

---

11   Hoffman, Phillipe and Kathryn Norberg (1994), Fiscal Crises, Liberty, and Representatives. Retrieved 21 January 2013

12   "OECD Revenue Statistics: 1965-2016".

1.4 History of Taxation in Africa

In many respects, the history of taxation in Africa is a story of external imposition of tax policies and practices, and of the influence of the global system and of the ideas of global epistemic communities of tax specialists. The origins of some contemporary tax practices lie in the colonial period, when the tax system was not only imposed externally but was fundamentally oriented to extraction and control. After independence, governments retained some of the features of colonial tax systems while introducing new and more 'modern' taxes from abroad. Two decades later, the period of structural adjustment brought major tax reforms dictated largely by the IMF and World Bank–including the introduction of VAT–with very little public debate. These external models were not always perfectly suited to local needs. In recent years, it has become increasingly clear that African countries are substantially–and negatively–affected by international tax rules over which they have no effective say.

More recently, there have been encouraging signs that African governments, civil society organizations and researchers are becoming more active and assertive in seeking to shape the future tax agenda on the continent. This is reflected in the creation of a new pan-African network of tax administrators, the African Tax Administration Forum (ATAF); in the development of closer tax cooperatives in Southern Eastern Africa, in the rise of civil society organizations and business associations that are increasingly engaged in shaping national tax debates; in African governments and civil society organizations finding a voice in international tax debates for sometime; and in the emergence of a distinctively African discussion of tax policy and administration dealing with issues as diverse as the taxation of small informal firms, approaches to more effectively taxing elites , and the use of mobile technology to improve taxation. The strength of local dialogue around tax reforms appears to us to be an essential part of any account of taxation in Africa and to be pivotal in the potential for long-term improvements.[13]

South Sudan was not an exception when it was part of Sudan. Application of taxation in South Sudan dates back to an unknown date during the Turkish rule of Mohammed Ali Pasha, and this is supported by what is written by Santandrea (1964) that "Ngiri-subsection of Kresh-They used to pay tribute to Chief Morjan Tule, until they became subjects of the Forege, after Zande and Mahdist invasions (1895)."[14]

The records in the same reference show that taxation existed since 1926 as stated that "NGabandala or Mandala or Bandala-a list of 1926 shows 560 Bandala taxpayers."[15]

1.5 Forms of Taxation

There are different historical forms of taxation since its inception and they are:[16]

1. **Corvée**: It refers to a person being forced to work instead of paying taxes. Such systems require certain classes of people to labour for a certain length of time, and the person would be free once the Corvée obligations were met. While a form of a free labour, it is also considered a tax, since a person's labour has value. Corvée was often implemented in areas

---

13   Mick Moore, Wilson Prichard and Odd-Helge F. Jeldstad. Op. cit. Pp. 13-14.

14   Santandrea, P. Stefano. A Tribal History of the Western Bahr El Ghazal. Italy, 1964. p. 197.

15   Ibid. p. 156.

16   Wikipedia, the free encyclopedia.

where the poor had no money to pay as taxes.

2. **Seigniorage**: The tax on creation of money. It is a profit or revenue taken from the minting of coins, usually the difference between the value of the bullion used and the face value of coin. In other words Seigniorage is the difference between the value of money and the actual cost required to produce it. Mints make a profit from this difference in value, so it is frequently viewed as a tax.

3. **Scutage**: It was a tax levied in England. A person could pay Scutage instead of serving in the military. It is a feudal tax paid in lieu of military service.

4. **Tallage**: Is a tax on land levied in Medieval Europe. It is an occasional tax levied by the Anglo-Norman Kings on crown lands and royal towns on feudal dependents.

5. **Tithe**: It is a tenth part of one's annual income, either in kind or money, contributed voluntarily for charitable purposes or due as tax for the support of clergy or Church. Tithe is a payment to a church or similar authority. While voluntary in modern times, historically these payments have been mandatory.

6. **Feudal (aids)**: A type of tax or due that was paid by a vassal to his lord during feudal times.

7. **Danegeld**: It was a tax paid to the Vikings to ensure the Vikings would not raid a person's land. Danegeld was a medieval land tax originally raised to pay off raiding Danes and later used to fund military expenditures. It was a tax levied in England from 10th to the 12th century to finance protection against Danish invasion.

8. **Carucage**: It was a tax on land levied in Medieval England. The tax was only collected when the government required extra revenue and was never levied regularly. It was a tax

which replaced the Danegeld in England.

9. **Socage**: A feudal tax system based on land rent. It was a feudal tenure of land by a tenant not a knight, in return for agricultural or other nonmilitary services or for payment of rent in money.

10. **Burgage**: A feudal tax system based on land rent. It was tenure in England and Scotland under which property of the King or a lord in a town was held for a yearly rent.

11. **Adet-i ağnam**: It was an annual tax on sheep and goats levied by the Ottoman Empire. Unlike most Ottoman taxes, this tax went to the national treasury, rather than regional treasuries. It was largely collected through tax farming.

12. **Resm-i arusane:** known as the bride tax, was a tax on marriage levied by the Ottoman Empire.

13. **Ravakçesi:** A tax levied on rabbis by the Ottoman Empire.

14. **Kharaj**: It was an Islamic tax on agricultural land.

15. **Window Tax**: It was a tax levied in England based on the number of windows on a building.

16. **Salt Tax:** It was a tax on salt. Salt taxes have been the least popular taxes in history. Salt taxes in France, India and Russia were significant contributors to revolutions or uprisings in those countries.

17. **Fiscus Judaicus:** It was a tax that Jews were required to pay in the Roman Empire.

18. **Leibzoll**: It was a tax that Jews were required to pay in Medieval Europe.

19. **Temple Tax:** It was a Roman tax used to pay for temples.

20. **Tolerance Tax:** It was a tax levied in Germany against Jews.

21. **Khums**: It was a tax on items looted during war levied in Islamic States.

In the colonial times, taxes in South Sudan were paid in form of men (slaves), ivory, gold, copper, livestock, crops or honey and any valuable ornament. To substantiate this statement, A. B. Theobald (1962) wrote that "the government took cattle from the nomads as taxes."[17] He continued that "There was only one compensation-the opportunity to get rich quickly. But having lined their own pockets, they still had to meet the demands of Cairo. This could only be done, firstly, by levying excessive taxation, and collecting it by force from the terrified people; and secondly, by exploiting the newly opened regions of the White Nile and Bahr El Ghazal for slaves and ivory."[18] The main purpose that ..."the Turko-Egyptian Government... originally went to the Sudan was with the conscious intention of exploiting it for slaves and gold."[19]

Theobald further revealed that "If they (the Sudanese) wish to grow corn they must pay for permission to do so, pay for liberty to take water from the broad Nile (without which the land is a sand desert), and pay for liberty to sell the corn. If the crop is good, pay double taxes (one for the private purse of the Pasha and one for the Government at (Cairo). If they don't grow corn they can't pay the taxes at all, and are kourbashed (good hippopotamus hide) and put into prison."[20]

At the time of the Mahdi's regime, "there was the 'Bait al-Mal' which was both the central treasury and the store of the Mahdi's government; for the proceeds of taxation (which was often paid

---

17   Theobald. A. B. The Mahdiya: A History of the Anglo-Egyptian, 1881-1899. Longmans, Green and Co. Ltd., London, Great Britain, 1962.

18   Ibid. p. 11.

19   Ibid. p. 26.

20   Ibid. p. 25.

in kind), captured loot and confiscated property were all deposited there."[21]

Santandrea (1964) also wrote thus "A number of tribesmen are settled in the districts of Sultans Ahmed Fartak (Raga) and Nasr Andal (Kossinga), and pay tribute in ivory to these sultans.[22] He further stated the collection from Belanda that "…the quantity of honey produced there is fabulous. They used to throw the wax away but now it forms part of the tax to the Government."[23]

Today there are regulations on taxation. Governments in more advanced countries (economies) i.e. Europe and North America tend to rely more on direct taxes, while developing economies i.e. India and several African countries rely more on indirect taxes.[24]

1.6 Objectives of Taxation

There are several objectives of taxation and they are:

1. **Economic Development**: One of the main objectives of taxation is economic development. Economic development of any country is largely conditioned by the growth of capital formation. It is said that capital formation is the kingpin of economic development. But LDCs usually suffer from the shortage of capital.

. To overcome the scarcity of capital, governments of these countries mobilize resources so that a rapid capital formation takes place. To step up both public and private investment, government taps tax revenues. Through proper tax planning,

---

21   Ibid. p. 46.

22   Santandrea. Op. cit. Pp. 183-184.

23   Ibid. p. 183.

24   William, J. McCluskey; Riël C. D. Franzsen (2005). Land value Taxation; An Applied Analysis. Ashgate. P. 73.

the ratio of savings to national income can be raised. By raising the existing rate of taxes or by imposing new taxes, the process of capital formation can be made smooth. One of the important elements of economic development is the raising of savings-income ratio which can be effectively raised through taxation policy.

. However, proper care has to be taken, regarding investment. If final resources or investments are channelized in the unproductive sectors of the economy, the economic development may be jeopardized even if savings and investment rates are increased. Thus, the tax policy has to be employed in such a way that investment occurs in the productive sectors of the economy, including the infrastructural sectors.

2. **Full Employment**: Second objective is full employment. Since the level of employment depends on effective demand, a country desirous of achieving the goal of full employment must cut down the rate of taxes. Consequently, disposable income will rise and, hence, demand for goods and services will rise. Increased demand will stimulate investment leading to a rise in income and employment through the multiplier mechanism.

3. **Price Stability**: Thirdly, taxation can be used to ensure price stability-a short run objective of taxation. Taxes are regarded as an effective means of controlling inflation. By raising the rate of direct taxes, private spending can be controlled. Naturally, the pressure on the commodity market is reduced. But indirect taxes imposed on commodities fuel inflationary tendencies. High commodity prices, on the one hand, discourage consumption and, on the other hand, encourage saving. Opposite effect will occur when taxes are lowered down during deflation.

4. **Control of Cyclical Fluctuations**: Fourthly, control of cyclical fluctuations-periods of boom and depression is considered to be another objective of taxation. During depression, taxes are lowered down while during boom taxes are increased so that cyclical fluctuations are tamed.

5. **Reduction of Balance of Payments (BOP) Difficulties**: Fifthly, taxes like custom duties are also used to control imports of certain goods with the objective of reducing the intensity of balance of payments difficulties and encouraging domestic production of import substitutes.

6. **Non-Revenue Objective**: Finally, another extra-revenue or non-revenue objective of taxation is the reduction of inequalities in income and wealth. This can be done by introducing a system of progressive taxation.

1.7 Purposes of Taxation

Taxation is used by the government for several other purposes which are:

1. To reduce pollution by taxing offending firms.
2. To discourage unhealthy lifestyle e.g. a tax on cigarettes.
3. To protect local and infant industries by taxing imports.
4. To achieve greater equality of wealth and income. Revenue from taxation is used to help the very poor e.g. providing food stamps.
5. To improve the balance of payments (BOP) by increasing the duties charged on imported goods.
6. To control spending in an economy thus reduce inflation.

1.8 Reasons for Taxation

There are several reasons why governments impose taxes. The reasons are as follows:[25]

1. **To Raise Revenue**: Most governments generally raise over 90% of the internally generated revenue from the different taxes. Raising revenue is therefore one of the most important and obvious reasons for taxation. Various types of taxes are imposed so that government collects the required amount of revenue. Government requires such tax revenue to finance public expenditure on education, health, defense, infrastructure and the general administration of the state.

2. **To Redistribute Income**: Naturally, income inequality exists between individuals and regions but if the income gap between the rich and the poor is very wide, it imposes serious consequences on the economy. Taxation redistributes a country's wealth by imposing a heavier tax burden on the rich in order to fund services for the poor. The very poor may even be exempted from certain forms of taxes. It is in relation to this that a tax threshold is set so that people earning below a given level of income are exempted from certain taxes. For purposes of redistributing incomes, progressive taxes are most appropriate.

3. **To Control Inflation**: Taxation withdraws money from public hands which have the effect of reducing demand and hence reducing inflation. During times of inflation, tax rates are raised so as to reduce purchasing power. Direct taxation on income is the most appropriate for this purpose.

4. **To Control Monopoly Power**: To control monopolies,

---

25   Mutamba, A. H. MK Fundamental Economics. East Africa Edition, MK Publishers, Kampala, Uganda, 2009. pp. 240-262.

governments impose specific, lump sum and profit taxes. Taxes imposed on monopolies reduce the abnormal profits enjoyed by such monopolists and hence reduce their dominance of the market.

5. **To Protect Domestic Infant Industries**: Infant industries need protection until they are able to withstand competition. Taxes on imports provide protection to infant industries. High taxes on imported products discourage imports and give the local infants industries a chance to expand and develop.

6. **To Discourage Dumping**: Dumping is the selling of a product at a cheaper price in a foreign market than in the home market. Dumping may destroy industries in the country where goods have been dumped. Taxes on such goods increase their prices such that they do not out compete local products. Taxation therefore helps control dumping.

7. **Control Consumption of Undesirable Commodities**: The government may consider certain commodities undesirable for consumption. Taxes are used to modify consumption patterns of people and therefore discourage or encourage the consumption of certain commodities. High taxes increase prices and discourage consumption. For example, a high excise duty is used to discourage alcohol consumption. Similar taxes may exist on cigarettes, pornographic materials, etc. The government therefore uses taxes to discourage the consumption of such commodities since it is very difficult to enforce a direct ban on their consumption.

8. **To Direct Investment and Resource Allocation**: Taxes are used as a tool to direct investment to desired sectors. Taxes on specific activities are indicators that investments in

such sectors or regions is no longer a priority while tax exemptions and tax holidays act as indicators of what the government is interested in and is likely to support. Tax revenue can also be used to subsidize and promote strategic sectors of the economy.

9. **To Correct Balance of Payments Problems**: Balance of payments problems exist when a country persistently exports less than what it imports, implying that, more funds are flowing out of the country than what is flowing into the country. Taxes on imports limit the consumption of imported products and hence reduce imports. By reducing imports, taxes help improve the balance of payments position of a country.

10. **Strengthening Foreign Relations**: Imposing taxes or removing existing taxes acts as a tool of promoting foreign relations among countries. By removing taxes on trade with a particular country, trade and bilateral relations with that country are promoted while imposing more taxes on trade with a specific country leads to reduction in economic cooperation and trade.

11. **Internalize External Costs**: In the process of production, certain firms transfer negative costs of production to the community. For example, a factory may pollute a village. A tax imposed on the polluting firm is used to help clean the environment so that people are not disadvantaged because of the activities of a private producer.

12. **Protecting the Environment**: Government may put very high taxes on certain products and activities to protect the environment. Very high taxes on charcoal are intended to make charcoal very expensive and discourage its use as a means of saving environment. High taxes on such commod-

ities make them expensive and unaffordable by some people hence reducing their consumption.

1.9 Principles of Taxation

A tax system for achieving certain objectives chooses and adheres to certain principles which are termed its characteristics. A good tax system, therefore, is one which is designed on the basis of an appropriate set of principles, such as equality and certainty. Mostly, however, objectives of taxation conflict with each other and a compromise is needed. Therefore, usually economists select some important objectives and work out the corresponding principles which the tax system[26] should adhere to.

Principles of taxation, alternatively called the canons of taxation or maxims of taxation are the standards government should follow when levying, collecting and administering a tax. The principles of taxation attempt to define the characteristics of a good tax. A tax that meets these guidelines is considered to be a good tax. The first set of four principles of taxation were enunciated by Adam Smith in 1776, which he called Canons of Taxation. Other economists have added and modified these principles of taxation. When taxes are imposed certain conditions must be fulfilled. The conditions are known as principles or canons of taxation. Therefore, the principles of taxation are:

1. Canon of Equality/Equity/Fairness: This canon tries to observe the objective of economic justice. It dictates that in absolute terms the richer should pay more taxes because without the protection of the State they could not have

---

26   Bhatia. Op. cit. p. 40.

earned and enjoyed that extra income.[27]

A good tax should be fair. Economists consider two principles to determine whether the burden of a tax is distributed fairly. They use the ability-to-pay principle and the benefit principle to determine fairness of a tax. The ability-to-pay principle states that taxes should be based on people's ability to pay, as measured by their income or wealth. The implication of this is that there should be horizontal and vertical equity in taxation. Horizontal equity means that people in equal positions or people with equal wealth and income should pay the same amount of tax. Vertical equity means that people with different abilities to pay (income) should pay different taxes. In short, similar people in terms of income should pay the same taxes while different people in terms of income should pay different taxes.[28]

The canon of equality, equity or justice is the most important canon of taxation. Smith explained it thus: "The subjects of every state ought to contribute towards the support of the government, as nearly as possible, in proportion to the revenue which they respectively enjoy under the protection of the state." It means that every person should pay the tax according to his ability and not the same amount. It also means that everybody should not pay at the same rate. Rather, every taxpayer should pay the tax in proportion to his income. The rich should pay more and at a higher rate than the other persons whose income is less. Thus this canon implies equality of sacrifice or ability to pay the tax in proportion to his income.[29]

---

27   Ibid. p. 41.

28   Mutamba. Op.cit. pp. 240-262.

29   Saleemi.Op. cit. pp. 8-9.

2. Canon of Certainty: This canon is meant to protect the taxpayers from unnecessary harassment by the "tax officials." The tax which individual is bound to pay ought to be certain, and not arbitrary. The time of payment, the quantity to be paid, ought all to be clear and plain to the contributor, and to every other person. The tax payers should not be subjected to arbitrariness and discretion of the tax officials, since that breeds a corrupt tax administration. With a scope for arbitrariness even honest tax machinery will become unpopular.[30] The tax imposed should be certain to the taxpayers and the tax administrators. The following must be certain to both parties:[31]

a) Who is liable to that tax.

b) How the tax is calculated.

c) When the tax is to be paid.

d) How the tax is to be paid.

e) The penalty for default.

f) What is being taxed (tax base).

Certainty is important to avoid conflict between taxpayers and tax collectors. According to Smith, there should be certainty in taxation because uncertainty breeds corruption. By the canon of certainty he means that "the tax which each individual is bound to pay ought to be certain, and not arbitrary. The time of payment, the manner of payment, the quantity to be paid ought all to be clear and plain to the contributor and to every other person." Thus this canon requires that there should be no element of arbitrariness in a tax. It should be clear to every taxpayer as to what, when, and where the tax is to be paid. Nothing should be left to

---

30   Bhatia.Op. cit. p. 42.

31   Mutamba. Op. cit. pp. 240-262.

the discretion of the income tax department. Certainty also means that the state should also be certain about the amount of tax revenue and the time when it is expected to flow in the Ministry of Finance.[32]

3. Canon of Convenience: The mode and timings of tax payment should be, so far as possible, convenient to the taxpayer. This canon recommends that unnecessary trouble to the taxpayer[33] should be avoided; otherwise various ill-effects may result.[34] A good tax system should be convenient to the taxpayer in terms of:[35]

a)Place of payment: The place of payment should be as near as possible to the taxpayer. If the tax collection agencies do not have offices nearby, they should appoint local agents or banks to collect taxes on their behalf.

b) Time of payment:The taxpayer should pay the tax when she/he has income. For example, salary earners should pay the tax at the end of the month and farmers after harvesting their crops.

c) Method of payment: Cash, cheques and other methods of payment convenient to the taxpayer should be acceptable. Payment should be in a readily available currency.

The canon of convenience lays down that both the time and manner of payment should be convenient to the taxpayer. In the words of Smith, "Every tax ought to be levied at the time or in the manner in which it is most likely to be convenient for the contributor to pay." The payment

---

32   Saleemi.Op. cit. p. 9.

33   Bhatia.Op. cit. p. 42.

34   Ibid. p. 42.

35   Mutamba. Op. cit. pp. 240-262.

of sales tax and excise duty by the consumer is convenient because he pays these taxes when he buys commodities and at a time when he has the means to buy. The manner of payment is very convenient to him because these taxes are included in the prices of commodities.[36]

4. Canon of Simplicity: A good tax should be simple for the taxpayer and the tax administrator. It should not be complicated to be understood by the taxpayer and tax collector. A simple tax compliments the principle of certainty. When the tax is simple to understand, it becomes more certain to the tax payers.[37]

The tax system should not be complicated. That makes it difficult to understand and administer and breeds problems of interpretation and legal disputes.[38]

The tax system should be simple, plain and intelligible to the common taxpayer. It should be simple to understand as to how is it to be calculated and how much is it to be paid. The form (s) to be filled up for calculation and payment of tax should be simple and intelligible to the taxpayer. This canon is essential in order to avoid corruption and oppression on the part of the tax department.[39]

5. Canon of Elasticity: This canon is closely related to that of productivity. The canon of elasticity requires that the government should be able to raise the rates of taxes when it is in need of more revenue. In other words, taxes should be elastic. The best example is excise duties. They can be levied on any

36   Saleemi.Op. cit. p. 9.

37   Mutamba. Op. cit. pp. 240-262.

38   Bhatia.Op. cit. p. 42.

39   Saleemi.Op. cit. p. 9.

number of commodities and their rates can be increased every year in order to raise more revenue. But care has to be taken that the rates of excise duties should not be so raised that they may encourage inflation pressures in the economy. [40]

The tax should not be rigid but flexible such that in case of need, it can be adjusted accordingly. The tax should also change in response to changes in the incomes of the taxpayers.[41] It should be possible for the authorities without undue delay, to revise the tax structure, both with respect to its coverage and rates, to suit the changing requirements of the economy and of the Treasury.[42]

6. The Canon of Flexibility: Flexibility in taxation is different from elasticity. Flexibility means that there should be no rigidity in taxation. The tax system can be changed to meet the revenue requirements of the state. On the other hand, elasticity in taxation means that the revenues can be increased under the prevailing tax system. But there cannot be any elasticity in taxation without flexibility because some change is required in the rates and structure of taxes if the state wants to increase revenue.[43]

7. Canon of Economy/cheapness: A good tax should be cheap to assess, collect, and administer. Government incurs expenses in tax administration, in collecting data, assessing taxpayers, paying wages and salaries to tax collectors, printing receipts and forms, paying bank charges and conducting tax

---

40   Saleemi.Op. cit. p. 9.

41   Mutamba. Op.cit. pp. 240-262.

42   Bhatai.Op. cit. p. 42.

43   Saleemi.Op. cit. p. 10.

education. An economical tax system ensures that these costs are as low as possible in comparison to the tax yields. The total costs incurred should not in any case exceed 5% of the total tax revenue. Compliance costs to the taxpayer should also be as low as possible. Taxpayers spend money to comply with the tax in terms of transport, telephone calls, payments to tax consultants and auditors. A good tax should minimize such compliance costs.[44]

This canon recommends that the cost of collection of taxes should be the minimum possible. It is useless to impose taxes which are too widespread and difficult to administer. These taxes entail unnecessary burden upon the society in the form of additional administrative expense.[45]

Every tax should satisfy the canon of economy in two ways. First, it should be economical for the state to collect it. If the cost of collection in the form of salaries of tax officials is more than what the tax brings as a revenue, such a tax is uneconomical, and hence it should not be levied. Second, it should be economical to the tax payer. It means that he should have sufficient money left with him after paying the tax. A very tax on incomes will discourage saving and investment, and thus adversely affect the production capacity of the community. Smith states this canon in these words: "Every tax ought to be so contrived as both to take out and to keep out of the pockets of the people as little as possible, over and above what it brings into public treasury of the state."[46]

8. Canon of Efficiency: The tax imposed should have lit-

---

44   Mutamba. Op. cit. pp. 240-262.

45   Bhatia. Op. cit. p. 42.

46   Saleemi. Op. cit. P. 9.

tle excess burden. Excess burden is the change in behavior caused by taxes. A tax imposed may make people to buy less of the taxed goods and more of the untaxed goods. The bigger the excess burden of a tax, the less efficient the tax is.[47]

9. Canon of Productivity: It is also called the canon of fiscal adequacy. According to this principle, the tax system should be able to yield enough revenue for the treasury and the government should have no need to resort to deficit financing.[48]

The productivity of a tax is its ability to achieve the purpose for which it is imposed. A tax imposed to raise revenue for government is productive when it raises sufficient and continuous revenue. A tax imposed to limit importation of certain products is productive if it succeeds in limiting the volume of imports of the targeted commodity.[49]

According to this canon, a tax should be productive in the sense that it should bring large revenue which should be adequate for the government. The government should tax people heavily. Such an effort would adversely affect the productive capacity of the economy. Further, this canon implies that one tax which brings large revenue is better than a number of taxes which bring small revenue. Many taxes may not be productive. They may also be uneconomical.[50]

10. Canon of Buoyancy: The tax revenue should have an inherent tendency to increase along with an increase in national income, even if the rates and coverage of taxes are not revised.[51]

---

47   Mutamba. Op. cit. pp. 240-262.

48   Bhatia. Op. cit. p. 42.

49   Mutamba. Op. cit. pp. 240-262.

50   Saleemi. Op. cit. p. 9.

51   Bhatia. Op. cit. p. 42.

11. Canon of Acceptability: A good tax should be socially, economically and politically acceptable. This depends largely on the level of tax education. If the taxpayers perceive the tax as oppressive and unjust, it causes resentment not only against the tax but also against the government that has imposed it. Unacceptable taxes have been the cause of coups and revolutions world over. A tax should therefore be weighed against the above principles to determine its suitability. A tax may score highly on one principle and score low on another. For example, a certain tax may be simple but not productive while another tax that is considered very convenient and equitable is not flexible. Obtaining a balance is still a challenge faced by tax authorities in many developing countries.[52]

12. Canon of Neutrality: A good tax system should be neutral, it should minimize the distortion of relative prices so that the government is able to reduce the problems of income inequality and promote the general welfare of people. A tax system is composed of all the taxes in an economy. The tax system as a whole can be evaluated on its goodness in terms of:

a) Economy, that is how much, is spent on taxation in relation to total tax revenue.

b) Diversity, how comprehensive it is.

c) Simplicity. How simple the tax system is.

d) Flexibility/buoyancy.

e) Neutrality.

f) Optimality, relation between what governments collect as revenue and what services it provides to the public.

The difference between a single tax and tax system can be

---

52   Mutamba. Op. cit. pp. 240-262.

compared to a single student and a class. The characteristics of a good student are not the same as the characteristics of a good class. A class is made up of more than one student just like the tax system is made up of more than one tax.[53]

13. Canon of Diversity: It is risky for the State to depend upon too few a source of public revenue. Such a system is bound to breed a lot of uncertainty for the treasury. It is also likely to be inequitable as between different sections of the society. On the other hand, if the tax revenue comes from diversified sources, then any reduction in tax revenue on account of any one cause is bound to be very small. However, too much multiplicity of taxes is also to be avoided. That leads to unnecessary cost of collection and violates the canon of economy.[54]

There should be diversity or variety in taxation. A single or a few taxes would neither meet the revenue requirements of the state nor satisfy the canon of equity. There should, therefore, be a variety of taxes so that all citizens should contribute towards state revenues according to their ability to pay. There should be a variety of direct and indirect taxes. But a large multiplicity of taxes will be difficult to administer and hence uneconomical.[55]

1.10. Taxable Capacity

This is the extent to which an individual taxpayer is able to pay taxes imposed on him without affecting the standard of living he

---

53   Ibid. pp. 240-262.

54   Bhatia.Op. cit. p. 43.

55   Saleemi.Op. cit. p. 11.

is used to. For the economy as a whole, taxable capacity is the total amount of money that can be raised from taxation without causing adverse effects on the economy. Most developing countries still collect a small proportion of Gross Domestic Product (GDP) as tax. This may be in the range of 15 to 25% while some countries collect as much as 45% of GDP as taxes.

There are various reasons why less developed countries collect less revenue from taxation. The taxable capacity is low because of the following factors:

a. Low incomes.
b. Big subsistence sector.
c. Lack of data on personal incomes and economic activities.
d. High levels of income inequality.
e. Political instability.
f. Dominance of the agricultural sector.
g. Unemployment.
h. Low levels of investment.
i. Poor administration.
j. Ignorance about the importance of taxation.

1.11. Effects of Taxation

Economists have devoted considerable effort to studying the effects of taxes. In particular, they study how taxes affect people's behavior, including their choices in working, saving, consuming and investment. Effects of taxation are:

a. **Effects of Taxation on Labour Supply**: Taxes affect the labour supply by influencing people's decisions on whether to work hard or not. Suppose an individual earns SSP100 per day and the government imposes a 20% tax on each earnings, then after tax, the individual receives only SSP80 per day. The impact of such a tax is hard to predict. On one hand, the tax lowers the cost to the individual by not working. For each hour of leisure, the individual gives up only SSP80 instead of SSP100. In effect, leisure becomes cheaper, so the individual tends to consume more of it-that is, to work less. On the other hand, with a lower wage, the individual must work more hours to maintain the standard of living he or she had before the tax. Thus, the tax simultaneously leads to two effects on work in opposite directions.

b. **Effects of Taxation on Savings**: Savings is the portion of income that is not spent. When a tax is levied on interest or dividends, it reduces the reward for saving. For example, if an individual earns 10% interest on a savings amount and faces a 2% income tax rate, then he or she makes only 8% return and the other 2% goes to the government. This effect tends to reduce the amount of saving that an individual makes.

c. **Effects of Taxation on Physical Investment**: In effect, a tax on business income is a tax on the physical investment's returns. Such tax reduces the firm's income and the benefit of making investments. Business taxes therefore decrease the amount of physical investment made by businesses.

1.12. Problems of Taxation in Less Developed Countries (LDCs)

The process of taxation is faced with a number of problems. These relate to the nature of taxes, methods of assessment and collection, nature and attitude of the taxpayers and tax collectors, logistical and management problems. They include:

a. **Inadequate Skilled Tax Collectors**: Most tax collectors are not professionally trained to assess and collect taxes. This is particularly so, for the direct taxes where local authorities and chiefs assess and collect taxes. This causes over taxation, under taxation and arbitrary assessments.

b. **Corruption and Embezzlement**: Corrupt tax collectors are a big problem to taxation. They under assess; receive bribes to assess less than what a tax payer should pay and even misuse the collected funds. In other cases, they over assess leading to tax avoidance and evasion by the taxpayers. This leads to less revenue being collected from taxation.

c. **Lack of Sufficient Logistics**: Tax collectors lack computers to help analyze and store data, they lack vehicles to move to remote areas for tax collection and other logistics.

d. **High Rate of Evasion**: There is a very high rate of tax evasion. People refuse to declare incomes. While for import and export duties, people smuggle the goods across national borders so as to evade taxes. This is facilitated by corrupt tax officials.

e. **Political Interference**: Political interference in tax matters involves government officials using their positions to favour their companies from taxation. Well-connected business people may get tax holidays and exemptions influenced by their friends in government, e.g. in South Sudan, Vivacell was granted in 2005, ten years exemption from paying taxes by the then Minister of Telecommunications and Postal Services.

f. **Large Subsistence Sector**: A large subsistence sector with low incomes means that a large part of the economy cannot be taxed. This means little revenue is collected in form of taxes.

g. **Unstable and Scattered Population**: Much of the population is unstable and moves from place to place and therefore difficult to trace and tax.

h. **Narrow Tax Base**: There are few items that can be taxed because there are few people who earn substantial incomes for direct taxation. This makes it difficult for government to collect sufficient revenue. It should be noted that there is always high rate of unemployment of labour in LDCs which further narrows the tax base.

i. Lack of accurate information and statistics about peoples' incomes and economic activities.

j. **Inflation**: Because of inflation, expected benefits cannot be realized as money loses value.

k. **Insecurity**: Due to insecurity, some areas are not accessible to tax assessors and collectors.

l. **Poor Infrastructure**: Due to poor road networks and communication facilities tax assessors and collectors are unable to reach certain areas.

m. **Politicizing of Taxation**: Politicians during campaigns tend to use taxation as tool to get votes by promising to reduce or completely remove certain taxes. This reduces peoples' willingness to pay during and after elections.

n. **Language and Communication Barriers**: In many cases, tax laws, policies and terminologies are difficult to be understood by the local population or people who pay the taxes.

o. **Unemployment**: Most of the labour force is unemployed leading to low taxable capacity and low tax revenue.

p. **Over Taxation**: Sometimes governments impose taxes which are too high for individuals or firms to pay with ease, leading to high tax evasion and tax avoidance.

1.13. Policies to Improve Taxation in LDCs

It is the wish of every government to have an efficient tax system that causes minimum burden, achieves the intended objectives, raises sufficient revenue and has minimal opposition. Various suggestions have been advanced to improve taxation in LDCs. The following are some of these suggestions:

a. Expanding the tax base by encouraging foreign and domestic investors.
b. Intensive taxpayer education.
c. Improvement in infrastructure.
d. Training tax collectors.
e. Putting up stringent measures against corruption and improving accountability for tax revenues.
f. Encourage more indirect taxes that are difficult to evade.
g. Empower the anti-smuggling agencies.
h. Re-activate industrial courts/tax tribunals.
i. Diversify economy.
j. Better monitoring and supervision of both the tax payers and the tax collectors.
k. Improve the tax system by computerizing and professionalizing it.

1.14. Rules Governing International Taxation

The rules governing international taxation have largely been made by the more powerful states. Unsurprisingly, they have been broadly designed to benefit their creators or powerful interests located within them. Early debates about who had the right to tax the profits of the companies operating internationally centred on the distinction between 'residence countries' and 'source countries': that is, between the place where a company was owned ('residence') and the place (s) where it did the business and thus sourced its profits ('source'). At the time, most companies undertaking foreign investment were resident in one of what later became known as OECD countries or where subsidiaries of such companies. The rules were implicitly designed to enhance the taxing rights of those OECD/residence countries. A similar pattern emerged in the international arrangements for taxing very wealthy individuals. Wealthy individuals in both richer and poorer countries increasingly sought to place their wealth in foreign bank accounts, at least in part to avoid the reach of national governments. The owners of that wealth were often politically powerful. Provided that most of their wealth continued to move to and between bank accounts located in OECD countries and their dependencies, little effort was made to monitor or control these movements.[56]

Over time, OECD countries increasingly entered into bilateral tax treaties, which established additional rules about how the right to tax MNCs would be divided among signatory countries. These treaties were initially primarily between OECD and developing countries became increasingly common. Formally, these treaties were designed to reduce the risk that the profits of an MNC would be taxed twice, first in the source country and the residence country-double taxation. However, the risk of double taxation is now much reduced: the tax authorities of most residence countries allow companies incorporated there to deduct corporate income taxes paid in source countries from their final corporate income tax bill at home. Instead, the primary role of tax treaties has been to shape the respective taxing rights of resident and source countries, either by setting explicit limits on the taxes that can

---

56   Mick Moore, Wilson Prichard and Odd-Helge F. Jeldstad. Op. cit. P. 41.

be levied by source countries, or by creating loopholes and grey areas that are open for abuse (Hearson 2013; 2015).[57]

---

57   Ibid. Pp. 41-42.

Chapter Two

TAX

2.1. Introduction

A tax is derived from the Latin word *taxo*. It is a mandatory financial charge or some other type of levy imposed upon a taxpayer (who may be an individual or other legal entity) by a governmental organization in order to fund various public expenditures. A failure to pay, or evasion of or resistance to taxation, is punishable by law. Taxes consist of direct or indirect taxes and may be paid in money or as its labour equivalent. Most countries have a tax system in place to pay for public or common national needs and government functions. Some countries levy a flat percentage rate of taxation on personal annual income, some on a scale based on annual income amounts, and some impose almost no taxation at all, or a very low tax rate for a certain area of taxation. Some countries charge a tax both on corporate income and dividends; this is often referred to as double taxation as the individual shareholder(s) receiving this payment from the company will also be levied some tax on that personal income.

Taxes are important sources of public revenue. Any government's priority is the generation of revenue by means of which it can procure services and goods necessary for the performance of its functions. In the past, government sought to undertake this duty through numerous ways amongst which tributes and booty, feudal services, grants, aids, military duty and cultivation of crown lands are known to be the most prominent one. Later on, with civilization and the modernization of states, governments started to procure revenue indirectly by means of revenue collected in the form of money from the citizens of the state in which the government in question exercises its functions. Therefore, so long as a system of private property subsists, individuals must contribute from their property for the support of government. Such contributions are due from those citizens of a state over whom a government may directly exercise jurisdiction, as with respect to their property, or for whom any of its functions may be directly performed, as for the defense of their persons or property. All in all, from the point of view of the individual, tax is a contribution whereas from the point of view of the government tax is a collection or procurement.

2.2. Concept and Definition of a Tax
2.2.1. Concept of a Tax
The best way to understand the term is to state the fundamental idea of a tax and afterwards to note its leading characteristics. In simpler terms, "tax is a financial charge or other levy imposed

on an individual or a legal entity by government". . Taxes are a portion of private wealth, exacted from individuals by the State for the purpose of meeting the expenditure essential to carrying out the functions of government. Taxes are contributions from the national dividend; they must ultimately come out of the annual earnings of the nation. The private income of a nation is the index of the capacity of the people to pay taxes, since it is the real source of public revenue. Labour and wealth employed productively by individuals create a fund which can be drawn upon; hence, as Adam Smith urged, the importance of measures which remove restraints on production, and which tend to stimulate the enterprise of people. Though taxes were historically voluntary contribution toward the expenses of government, gradually they were transformed into obligatory actions. At the present time, payment of taxes is obligatory in all civilized nations. The bearer of the tax is in all cases a person. Taxes are burdens, or charges, imposed by "the legislative power of a state upon persons or property," to "raise money for public purposes." It is a power inherent in sovereignty, and without which constitutional government cannot exist. It is vested in the Legislature by the general grant of the legislative power whether specially enumerated in the Constitution among the powers to be exercised by it or not.

A tax is a compulsory contribution of persons toward the needs of government. It follows from this definition: that a tax involves coercion upon its bearers; who are in every case, either natural or legal persons; and, a specific public purpose as its end.

A tax is not a price paid by the taxpayer for any definite service rendered or a commodity supplied by the government. The benefits received by taxpayers from the government are not related to or based upon their being taxpayers. A tax is a generalized exaction, which may be levied on one or more criteria upon individuals, groups of individuals, or other legal entities.[58]

2.2.2. Definition of a Tax

A number of authors have tried to define the term 'tax'; however, it is hard to say that these attempts at coming up with a definition for the term have been successful, mainly owing to the fact that too great precision is attempted in a single sentence. There are different legal and economic definitions of a tax. Some of the definitions are as follows:

1. Accordingly, in general terms, tax can be defined as a contribution from individuals out of their private property for the maintenance and defense of government, so that it may perform its functions and the ends of the state be realized.

2. From the view point of economists, a tax is a non-penal, yet compulsory transfer of resources from the private to the public sector levied on a basis of predetermined criteria and without reference to specific benefit received.

3. A tax can be defined as a payment to support the cost of government. A tax differs from a fine or penalty imposed by the government because a tax is not intended to deter or punish unacceptable behaviour. On the other hand, taxes are compulsory rather than voluntary on the part of the payer. A tax differs from a user's fee because the payment of a tax does not entitle the payer to a specific good or service in return.[59]

4. A tax is a compulsory levy payable by an economic unit to the government without any corresponding entitlement to

---

58   Bhatia. Op. cit. p. 37.

59   Sally M. Jones and Sheley C. Rhoades-Catanach. Principles of Taxation for Business and Investment Planning, 2008 Edition, Mc Graw-Hill, Irwin.

receive a definite and direct quid pro quo from the government.

5. A tax is a compulsory payment levied on the persons or companies to meet the expenditure incurred on conferring common benefits upon the people of a country.

6. Taxes are the most important source of government income. Dr. Dalton defined a tax as "a compulsory contribution imposed by a public authority, irrespective of the exact amount of service rendered to the taxpayer in return."[60]

7. According to Professor Seligman, a tax is "a compulsory contribution from a person to the government to defray the expenses incurred in the common interest of all, without reference to special benefits conferred."[61]

8. Tax may be also defined as a compulsory contribution of wealth of a person or body of persons for the services of public powers. It means taxes are a portion of the produce of the land, a labour of the country placed at the disposal of the government.[62]

9. A tax is an involuntary payment made by individuals or businesses to a state, or to functional equivalents of a state.

10. A tax is also defined as a compulsory contribution collected by government for public use.

From the definitions above, the following should be noted:[63]

1. Only the central or regional government or a functional equivalent of a government can levy and collect taxes. A

---

60   Saleemi.Op. cit. p. 3.

61   Ibid. p. 3.

62   Ibid. p. 4.

63   Mutamba. Op. cit. pp.240–262.

company, individual person, or private organization cannot levy and collect taxes. This should not be confused with situations when the government contracts private companies to collect taxes on its behalf.

2. Taxes are non-quid pro quo payments, that is, they are not value-for-value payments. A taxpayer cannot demand an exact amount of goods or services from government in direct exchange for the taxes paid.

3. Taxes are compulsory. Once levied, they have to be paid.

2.3. Characteristics of a Good Tax System

The characteristics of a tax are as follows:

1. First, it is a compulsory payment imposed by the government of the people residing in the country. Since it is a compulsory payment, a person who refuses to pay a tax is liable for punishment. But a tax is to be paid only by those who come under its jurisdiction. Similarly, persons who buy a commodity which carries a tax on it, pay the tax while others do not.

2. Second, a tax is a payment made by the taxpayers which is used by the government for the benefit of all the citizens. The state uses the revenue collected from taxes for providing the hospitals, schools, public utility services, etc. which benefit all people.

3. Third, a tax is not levied in return for any specific service rendered by the government to the taxpayer. An individual cannot ask for any special benefit from the state in return for the tax paid by him.

According to Professor Taussig, "The essence of a tax... is the absence of a direct quid pro quo between the taxpayer and the public authority. It implies that the taxpayer cannot claim something equivalent. In other words, you cannot refuse to pay a tax on the ground that you do not use a service. A rich man may be childless but he has to pay taxes spent on schools. Taxes are meant to cover the general expenses of the state and are not levied for any particular purpose. Hence, the government does not promise to perform a specific service in return for the payment for a particular tax"[64].

2.4. Essentials of an Optimum Tax System

A good tax system should be composed of taxes which conform to the main canons of taxation. The system as a whole should be equitable. Its burden should fall on the broadest shoulders. It should also be economical, so that the work of collection is done as cheaply as possible. It should not hamper the development of trade and industry. It should, on the other hand, assist the economic development of the country.[65] The government should be certain of its revenue. The tax system should be based on comprehensive and up-to-date statistical information so that accurate forecasting is made possible. The tax system should not be a mere leap in the dark. Its effects should be calculable with a reasonable precision. The taxes, as a whole, should be convenient, i.e. felt as little as possible.

The tax system should be simple, financially adequate and elastic so that it can respond to the new needs of the state.

The ideal of simplicity may lead us to advocate a single tax. But the single tax will expose the tax system to other serious objections. It, is therefore, agreed that a tax system should be as much broad-based as possible. There should be diversity in the

---

64   Ibid. p. 4

65   Saleemi. Op. cit. p. 14.

system. But we do not want too great multiplicity.

Further, the tax system should be efficient from the administrative point of view. It should be simple to administer. There should be little scope for evasion or accumulation of arrears. It should be fool-proof and knave-proof. Chances of corruption should be minimized.

Another important characteristic of a good tax system is that it should be harmonious whole. It should be truly a system and not a mere collection of isolated taxes. Every tax should fit in properly in the system as a whole so that it is a part of connected system. Each tax should occupy a definite and due place in the financial structure.

From the point of view of ensuring economic stability, it is necessary that the tax system must be progressive in relation to changes in national income.[66] This means that when national income rises, an increasing part of the rise in income should automatically accrue to the tax authorities and when national income falls, as in a depression, the tax revenue should fall faster than the fall of national income. This characteristic of the tax system will ensure that when national income is increasing, as during a boom, a large part of it is being drawn into the tax so as to moderate the rise in the purchasing power of the people, helping there by to keep the price rise in check. Similarly, in depression, tax revenues should fall faster than income so that people's purchasing power does not fall as faster as their pre-tax income. This will serve to moderate the extent of decline in economic activity during a depression.

Thus, an overall progressive tax system is an important factor in ensuring economic stability.

66   Ibid. p. 15.

For developing economics, the tax system has to serve as an instrument of economic growth. Economic development, rather than economic stability, is the objective of under-developed economies. Their tax system must be so shaped as to accelerate development. For this purpose, it must mobilize the country's resources and channelize them into desirable investments. It must, in short, step up saving and investment.

According to the Cambridge economist Kaldor, there are three main considerations that should be taken into account in framing an effective system, which are equity, economic effects, and administrative efficiency. From the point of view of equity, the most important consideration is that the tax system should not contain a systematic bias in favour of particular groups of taxpayers and against others. From the point of view of economic effects of taxation, the major consideration is to prevent the tax system from becoming too much of a disincentive on effort, initiative or enterprise. From the point of view of administrative efficiency, all loopholes for evasion should be plugged and the main requirements are: simplicity and comprehensiveness embracing all forms of beneficial receipt, a single comprehensive return, self-checking system of taxation and automatic reporting system.[67]

2.5. Purposes of Taxes

Taxes are mostly levied with the object of raising revenues. A penalty, on the other hand, is imposed to stop people from doing certain things. Sometimes a tax may be levied which does both. It may bring in some revenue and also check people from consuming some harmful articles like opium. Besides, certain taxes may be of the nature of protective duties. They are levied in or-

---

67   Ibid. p. 16.

der to protect some home industry against foreign competition. Sometimes a tax has another motive in view. It aims at removing the inequalities in the distribution of wealth in a society. Well-to-do people may be taxed to provide services like free schooling and free medical aid for the poor. Thus, raising revenue is not the only purpose for which taxes are levied.[68]

The main purposes of taxes are as follows:

1. **Raising Revenue**: The primary purpose of taxes "is to raise revenue for government expenditure."[69] The government needs money to maintain the peace and security in the country, to increase social welfare, to complete the developmental projects like roads, dams, power stations, etc. Taxes are considered the main source of public revenue.[70]

2. **Economic Stability**: Taxes are also imposed to maintain economic stability in the country. During inflation, the government imposes more taxes in order to discourage unnecessary expenditure of the individuals. Similarly, during deflation, taxes are reduced in order to enable the individuals to spend more money. In this way, the increase or decrease in taxes helps to check the big fluctuations in the prices and maintain the economic stability.[71]

3. **Fair Distribution of Income**: Taxes are also imposed to achieve the equality in the distribution of national income. Taxes are imposed at higher rates on rich persons and these amounts are spent to increase the welfare of poor persons. In

---

68   Ibid. p. 4.

69   Geoffrey Morse & David Williams. Davies: Principles of Tax Law. Fifth Edition, Sweet and Maxwell Ltd. London, England, 2004. Pp. 4-5.

70   Saleemi. Op. cit. p. 4.

71   Ibid. p. 5.

this way, taxes help to achieve the fair distribution of income in the country.

4. **Optimum Allocation of Resources**: Taxes are also imposed to allocate the resources of the country for optimum use of the resources. The amounts collected by the government from taxes are spent on more productive projects. It means the resources are allocated to achieve the maximum possible output in the given circumstances.

5. **Protection Policy**: Taxes are also imposed to implement the protection policy of the government. In order to give protection to those commodities which are produced in the country, the government imposes heavy taxes on the import of such commodities from other countries. In view of these taxes, the individuals are induced to buy local products.

6. **Social Welfare**: The government imposes taxes on the production of those commodities which are harmful for human health e.g. excises duty on wines, opium, cigarettes etc.

7. **Higher Employment Level**: The government also imposes taxes in order to complete some public works programmes. It means the government can solve the problem of unemployment to a great extent by starting new projects. In this way, taxes help to create more employment opportunities.[72]

2.6. Objectives of a Good Tax System

Taxes are imposed by the government to achieve some specific objectives. The imposition of taxes creates some burden on the individuals. The amounts collected by the government through taxes are spent for productive and welfare purposes. It means the taxes may create some good or bad effects. An optimum or

---

72   Ibid. p. 6.

good tax system may be defined as that tax system which helps to achieve maximum possible number of principles of taxation. A good tax system should also help to achieve the following objectives:[73]

1. To maintain economic stability.
2. To equalize the distribution of income.
3. To increase the rate of economic growth.

2.7. Types of Taxes

A business must pay a variety of taxes based on the company's physical location, ownership structure and nature of the business. Business taxes can have a huge impact on the profitability of businesses and the amount of business investment. Taxation is a very important factor in the financial investment decision-making process because a lower tax burden allows the company to lower prices or generate higher revenue, which can then be paid out in wages, salaries and/or dividends. Business may be required to remit the following types of taxes:

1. **Consumption Tax**: Is a tax on the money people spend, not on the money people earn.
2. **Value Added Tax (VAT) or Ad Valorem Tax**: Ad Valorem' is a Latin word meaning 'According to Value'. It is a tax on manufacturing that taxes the difference between the cost of raw materials and the cost of the final product. It is a national sales tax collected at each stage of production or consumption of a good. Depending on the political climate, the taxing authority often exempts certain necessary living items, such as food and medicine from the tax.
3. **Property Tax**: Many countries have Proper-

---

73   Ibid. p. 8.

ty tax, or millage tax. It is the tax which the owner pays on the value of the property being taxed. The taxing authority requires and/or performs an appraisal of the monetary value of the property, and tax is assessed in proportion to that value. Forms of property tax used vary between countries and jurisdictions. Taxes paid on homes, land or commercial real estate or other personal property. Property taxes are usually imposed by local governments and charged on a recurring basis. Other items that may be subject to property tax are automobiles, boats, recreational vehicles and airplanes. Some states include factories, wharves, etc.

4. **Capital Gains Tax**: Is a tax on the sale of an investment, usually stocks, bonds, precious metals and property. Capital gains tax is charged on the profit realized on the sale of a non-inventory asset that was purchased at a lower price. Not all countries implement a capital gains tax and most have different rates of taxation for individuals and corporations. Taxes on investment income after an investment are sold and a capital gain is realized. There are also taxes on dividends and interests stemming from simple interest from a bank account or dividends and earnings from investments. Paid on any profits made from the sale of an asset and are usually applied to stock and bond transactions. Profits made from the sale of real estate are also subject to capital gains tax.

5. **Inheritance/Estate Taxes**: A tax paid on money gained through inheritance. It is a tax imposed on the transfer of property upon the death of the owner. Taxes paid after someone dies. An estate tax is paid from the net worth of the deceased. It is a tax on the privilege of inheriting assets, and so is paid by the heir, not the estate of the deceased.

6. **Gift Tax**: a tax on gifts received.

7. **Payroll Taxes**: A tax an employer withholds and/or pays on behalf of their employees based on the wage or salary of the employee. In most countries, including the United States, both state and federal authorities collect some form of payroll tax. In the United States, Medicare and Social Security, also called FICA, make up the payroll tax. These taxes cover contribution of an employee to Medicare, to Social Security retirement, disability and survivor benefits and to unemployment benefits. There are other income taxes withheld from an employee pay check.

8. **Federal Income Tax:** A tax levied by a national government on annual income.

9. **State and/or Local Income Tax:** A tax levied by a state or local government on annual income. Not all states have implemented state level income taxes.

10. **Poll tax, also called a Head Tax**: is a fixed tax that must be paid by each person.

11. **Income Taxes**: Tax on money an individual earns. Is levied on personal and business revenue and interest income. Income tax brackets are progressive. Businesses pay taxes on their net income.

12. **Corporate/Corporation tax**: is levied on the earnings or profits of a corporation. This tax is levied on profits earned by companies. It is a proportional tax which is levied at the constant rate.

13. **Dividend Tax:** is a tax on dividends paid to shareholders of a company.

14. **Unemployment Tax**: A federal tax that is allocated to state unemployment agencies to fund unemployment assistance

for laid-off workers.

15. **Sales Tax**: It is a tax on retail sales. A tax imposed by the government at the point of sale on retail goods and services. It is collected by the retailer and passed on to the state. Sales tax is based on a percentage of the selling prices of the goods and services and is set by the state. Technically, consumers pay sales taxes, but effectively, business pay them since the tax increases consumers costs and causes them to buy less. Some believe that it is the most equitable form of tax since it is voluntary and extract more money from those who consume more. Also it is believed to be most regressive form of tax since poorer people wind up paying a larger proportion of their income in sales tax than wealthier individuals do.

16. **Foreign Tax**: Income taxes paid to a foreign government on income earned in that country.

17. **Excise Tax:** It is based on the quantity of an item and not on its value e.g. government imposes an excise tax of SSP20 on every gallon of gas purchased, regardless of the price charged by the seller. States often add an additional excise tax on each gallon.

18. **A tariff**: It is a tax levied on items crossing an international border.

19. **User Fees:** They are taxes assessed on a wide variety of services, including airline tickets, rental cars, toll roads, utilities, hotel rooms, licenses, financial transactions and many others. Depending on where someone lives, a cell phone, for example, may has as many as separate user taxes, running up monthly bill by much as 20 percent.

20. **Development Impact Tax**: It is a fee charged to a developer to pay for the amount of infrastructure that will need to be

built to accommodate the new residents or customers of the development. Such fees fund municipal government services such as roads, domestic water services and schools.

21. **Sin Tax**: It is a tax levied against any undesired activity. This includes taxes on alcohol and cigarettes. Luxury taxes are imposed on items such as expensive cars or jewelry.

22. **Jizya/Zakat**: Is a tax paid by non-Muslims or Muslims in a Muslim state.

23. **Alcoholic Tax**: It is a tax that levies alcohol.

24. **Carbon Tax:** Is a tax levied on the carbon content of fuels, as a measure to overcome the impact of global warming.

25. **Fat Tax**: Is a tax levied on unhealthy foods.

26. **Financial Transaction Tax**: Is a tax on certain financial transactions, such as the sale of stocks.

27. **Fuel Excise**: Is a tax levied on fuels, especially for motor vehicles.

28. **Luxury Tax**: Is a tax on luxury goods.

29. **Soda Tax**: Is a tax on soda.

30. **Stamp Duty**: Is a tax levied on official documents. Is a form of tax that is levied on documents relating to immovable property, stocks and shares. Apart from transfers of shares and securities, stamp duties are also charged on the issue of bearer instruments and certain transactions involving partnerships.

31. **Transfer Tax**: Is a tax levied on the sale of property.

32. **Vehicle Excise Duty:** Is a tax on vehicles levied in the United Kingdom.

33. **Per Unit Tax**: A tax charged proportionally to the amount sold, such as by cents per kilogram.

34. **Turnover Tax**: A tax on intermediate and capital goods that is viewed as a precursor to a value-added tax.

35. **Use Tax**: A tax charged on an item purchased in an area without a sales tax when brought to areas that has one.

36. **Petroleum Revenue Tax**: It is a tax levied on the profits of companies involved in drilling of oil and gas. This tax may or may not exist in other countries.

It is worthy to note that on one hand…"central government taxes such as personal income, corporate income tax, value added tax, customs duties and taxes on natural resources…provide the bulk of government revenue."[74]

On the other hand, "direct taxes on income and wealth are more likely to harvest revenue from relatively wealthy than are taxes on sales, imports or value added."[75]

2.8. Classification of Taxes

Tax is a compulsory contribution which is levied on the person to meet the expenses which are incurred for a common cause. Taxes may be classified on the basis of:[76]

1. **Impact of a Tax:** It means on whom tax is imposed and who is to bear the burden of the tax. In this case, the taxes may be:

    a. Direct taxes

    b. Indirect taxes.

    The classification of taxes into direct and indirect owes to the relationship between the nature of the taxes and the reason for payment of the taxes. A direct tax is one for which the formal and economic incidence are essentially the same, i.e.

---

74   Mick Moore, Wilson Prichard and Odd-Helge F. Jeldstad. Op. cit. p. 6.

75   Saleemi. Op. cit. p. 8.

76   Ibid. p. 18.

the taxpayer is not able to pass the burden to someone else. Accordingly, direct taxes are paid entirely by those persons on whom they are imposed. On the other hand, an indirect tax is a tax whereby the taxpayer's burden to pay the tax can easily be passed on to another person. Generally, the tax incidence of an indirect tax is on the ultimate consumer; however, sometimes, sellers might absorb such indirect taxes so as to be competitive in the market in which they are operating.

2. **Base of the Tax**: This is the economic activity, commodity or income upon which a tax is levied in order to raise tax revenue.[77] The tax base is the object upon which the tax is levied and to which the tax rate is applied. The base of a tax is the legal description of the object with reference to which the tax is payable. For example, the base of an excise tax is production, packing or processing of a specific good; the base of an income tax is the income of the assessee defined and estimated in terms of certain rules laid down for this purpose; a gift may be defined and made a base for levying a gift tax. The base of each tax has to be defined legally and it is to be quantified for the purpose of determining the tax liability of an individual taxpayer. Each taxpayer is considered a legal entity for this purpose. Accordingly, an individual legal entity may be subjected to more than one tax. It should be noted that a tax base may have a time dimension also. For example, income tax is usually on an annual basis and the law has to decide whether income would be taxed on the basis of accrual or receipt. The authorities, while determining a tax base, are expected to give due consideration to various questions like those of cost of collection, administration and

---

77   Mutamba. Op. cit. p. 258.

effects of that tax. The exact coverage of a tax base is sought to be determined by an optimum combination of these considerations. With the passage of time, a tax base under consideration may grow or may shrink. For example, as production of excisable goods increases, the base of excise duties also grows. Relevant provisions, definitions and rules of a tax may be changed to extend its coverage or base. Also, its coverage may be increased by bringing additional items under it.[78] In this case, the taxes may be:

a. **Income Tax**: The tax base is income.

b. **Property Tax**: The tax base is the property.

c. **Sales Tax**: The tax base is the sale price of goods sold.

d. **Export Tax**: The tax base is the value of goods exported.

e. **Import Tax**: The tax base is the value of goods imported.

3. **Rates of a Tax**: The rate of a tax is the percentage of the tax base to be taken in case of a tax. In this case, the taxes may be:

a. Progressive

b. Proportional

c. Regressive

d. Degressive.

---

78   Bhatia. Op. cit. pp. 39-40

Taxes are classified according to the types in the figure below:

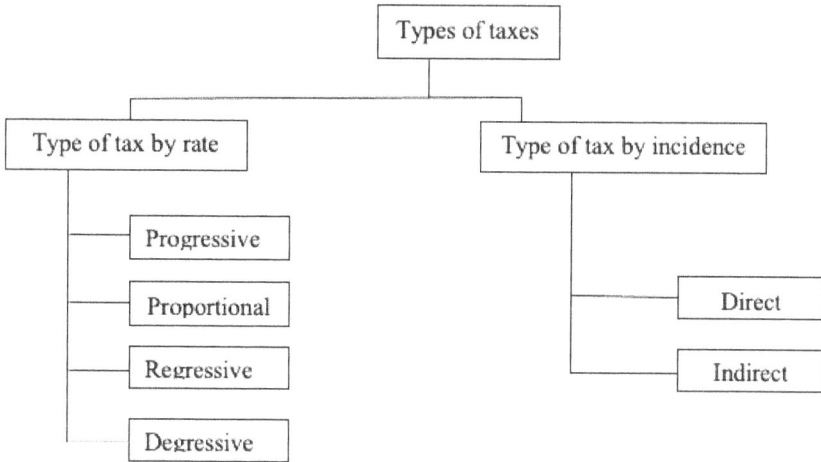

```
                          ┌──────────────┐
                          │ Types of taxes│
                          └──────┬───────┘
          ┌──────────────────────┴──────────────────────┐
┌──────────────────┐                        ┌──────────────────────┐
│ Type of tax by rate│                       │ Type of tax by incidence│
└─────────┬────────┘                        └──────────┬───────────┘
          │   ┌─────────────┐                           │
          ├───│ Progressive │                           │
          │   └─────────────┘                           │        ┌────────┐
          │   ┌─────────────┐                           ├────────│ Direct │
          ├───│ Proportional│                           │        └────────┘
          │   └─────────────┘                           │        ┌────────┐
          │   ┌─────────────┐                           └────────│ Indirect│
          ├───│ Regressive  │                                    └────────┘
          │   └─────────────┘
          │   ┌─────────────┐
          └───│ Degressive  │
              └─────────────┘
```

Governments impose many types of taxes. Individuals pay income tax when they earn, they pay consumption tax when they spend, and pay property taxes for houses or land that they own. These and all other taxes can be put into various categories depending on: Tax rate and Tax incidence.[79]

1. Under the tax rate classification, we have: Progressive tax, Proportional tax, Regressive tax and Degressive tax.
2. Under the incidence of tax classification, we have: Direct tax and Indirect tax.

2.9. Proportional, Progressive, Regressive and Degressive Taxes

Taxes have been variously classified. Taxes may be progressive, proportional, regressive and degressive.

1. Proportional Tax: A proportional tax is one in which, what–

---

79   Mutamba. Op. cit. pp. 246-258.

ever the size of income, same rate or same percentage is charged. If all the taxpayers have to pay, say one percent of their income as tax, it is a case of proportional taxation. The same percentage is charged from all taxpayers. The merit of proportional taxation is that it is much simpler than progressive taxation. But simplicity is not a very essential virtue in a tax. All modern governments have now adopted the principle of progression in direct taxation and proportional taxation in taxing commodities. The following hypothetical table and graph explain the point more clearly:

Tax Base	Tax Rate	Amount of Tax Payable
SSP 5,000	10%	SSP500
SSP10,000	10%	SSP1,000
SSP15,000	10%	SSP1,500
SSP20,000	10%	SSP2,000

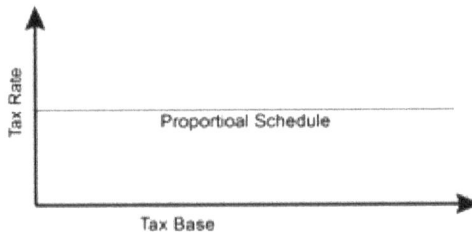

2. Progressive Tax: If, on the other hand, the rate of the tax rises as the taxable income increases, the tax is called a progressive tax. The principle of a progressive tax is: "the higher the income, the higher the rate." For instance, when income is divided into groups, the rate or percentage of taxation increases with the increase in income e.g. persons, say in the income bracket of SSP1,000–SSP1,500 pay at a given rate and persons in the income bracket of SSP1,501–SSP2,000 pay at a higher rate.[80] It is worth noting that even under a proportional tax the rich man pays more. For example, if the rate is 1% on the monthly salary, a man who is getting SSP1,000 will pay SSP120 per a year and the man who is getting SSP2,000 will pay SSP240 per a year. Thus, the man with the higher income pays more even under the proportional taxation. But under progressive taxation, he will pay much more because as income increases the rate of the tax must also increase. The man with SSP2,000 monthly salary may have to pay 2% instead of 1%. He will pay; therefore pay SSP480 instead of SSP240 per year. The following hypothetical table and graph explain the point more clearly:

Tax Base	Tax Rate	Amount of Tax Payable
SSP 5,000	10%	SSP500
SSP10,000	15%	SSP1,000
SSP15,000	20%	SSP1,500
SSP20,000	25%	SSP2,000

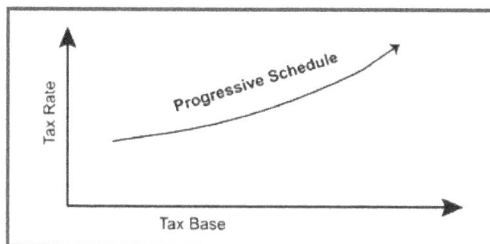

---

80   Saleemi. Op. cit. p. 27.

2.10. Merits of Progressive Tax

Progressive tax is justified on the following grounds:

a. It is more equitable. The broader shoulders are asked to carry the heavier burden.

b. It is productive. Its yield is much more than it would be under proportional taxation.

c. It is economical. Cost of collection does not increase with the increase in the rate of tax.

d. It brings about an equality of sacrifice among the taxpayers. This because the law of diminishing utility applies to money also. The marginal utility of money decreases with every increase in the income. Hence, the richer a man is, the less the sacrifice he feels in paying a certain tax. By taxing him/her more, he/she is asked to make equal sacrifice.

e. By means of progressive taxation, the inequalities of wealth distribution can be reduced to some extent. Moreover, fair distribution of wealth will result in increased welfare of the community, because the rich will sacrifice only their luxuries, while the poor men will be able to satisfy their wants a little more fully.

2.11. Demerits of Progressive Tax

Progressive tax, however, is subjected to the following criticism:

a. If it is very heavy, it will discourage savings. Less capital will be accumulated, and productive capacity of the community will be impaired.

b. It is all arbitrary.

c. It is based on the assumption that the same amount of money means the same utility to all taxpayers with equal incomes. This is actually not so, because circumstances of individual taxpayers are widely different.

d. It is very inconvenient and pinches the taxpayers very much.

3. Regressive Tax: A tax is said to be regressive when its burden falls more heavily on the poor than on the rich. It is the opposite of a progressive tax. No civilized government imposes a tax in which, as income increases, the rate of tax is lowered. That would be clearly unjust. But there are several taxes on commodities whose burden rests mainly on the poor.

The following hypothetical table and graph explain the point more clearly:

Tax Base	Tax Rate	Amount of Tax Payable
SSP 5,000	12%	SSP600
SSP10,000	9%	SSP900
SSP15,000	7%	SSP1,050
SSP20,000	6%	SSP1,200

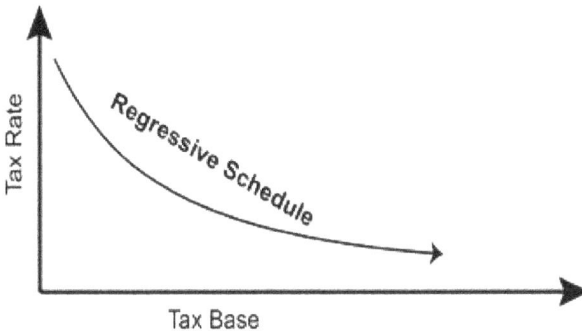

4. Degressive Tax: The tax is called degressive when the higher incomes do not make a due contribution or when the burden imposed on them is relatively less. This will happen when a tax is only mildly progressive, i.e. when the rate of progression is not sufficiently steep. A tax may be progressive up to a limit beyond which the same rate is charged. In that case, there may be lower relative sacrifice for the larger incomes than for the smaller incomes.

Another way in which a degressive tax may occur is when the highest percentage is set for that given type of income on which it is intended to exert more pressure; and from this point onwards, the rate is applied proportionally on higher incomes and decreasingly on lower incomes, falling to zero on the lowest incomes.[81]

The following hypothetical table and graph explain the point more clearly:

Tax Base	Tax Rate	Amount of Tax Payable
SSP 5,000	10%	SSP500
SSP10,000	11%	SSP1,100
SSP15,000	12%	SSP1,800
SSP20,000	13%	SSP2,600
SSP30,000	13%	SSP3,900

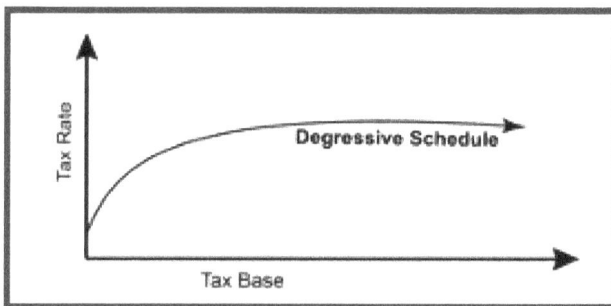

---

81   Ibid. p. 29.

2.12. Other Types of Taxes According to Tax Rates

1. **Average Rate of Tax**: The average rate (effective rate of tax) is the total tax paid divided by the total value of the product or income on which the tax is based. That is, tax paid divided by the taxable income. It is calculated as:

    Average rate of tax = $\frac{\text{tax paid}}{\text{Income taxed}}$

    For example, if the tax rate is 5% of income, then it means the tax payer who earns 2,500SSP will pay 5% of it as tax that is 125SSP.

2. **Marginal Tax Rate**: The marginal tax rate is the rate paid on each extra South Sudanese Pound of income earned. Marginal rate of tax is calculated as change in taxes divided by change in income.

    Marginal rate of tax = $\frac{\text{Change in taxes}}{\text{Change in income}}$

    In classifying taxes, average rate of tax is used.

3. **Specific Taxes**: A specific tax is imposed as a given amount of tax per unit of output irrespective of the value of that unit. It is expressed in monetary units per unit of output. For example, a tax of SSP2 per loaf of bread produced is a specific tax. Every loaf of bread is charged SSP2 irrespective of its cost. An example of specific tax is excise duty.

4. **Ad Valorem Taxes**: The tax value is expressed as a percentage of the value of the commodity. This means that as the price of the commodity changes, the tax also changes along. For example, if a tax of 10% is imposed on each bottle of soda and a soda cost SSP4, it means the tax will be 10% of SSP4 which is 40 piastres. If the price of soda increases to SSP180, the tax will be 10% of SSP180 which is SSP18.

2.13. Direct and Indirect Taxes

Direct and indirect taxes are usually defined on the basis of the impact and incidence of the tax.

Direct tax is the tax under which the impact and incidence is on the same person e.g. income tax and death duty.

Indirect tax is that tax under which the impact of the tax is on one person and incidence is on the other person e.g. excise duty, custom duty, sales tax etc. By impact of tax, we mean on whom tax is imposed. Incidence of tax means who is to bear the burden of the tax.

According to Dalton, "A direct tax is really paid by the person on whom it is legally imposed, while an indirect tax is imposed on one person, but paid partly or wholly by another."

John Stuart Mill defined a direct tax as one which is "demanded from the very person who it is intended or desired as one which is demanded from one person in the expectation and intended that he/she shall indemnify himself/herself at the expense of the another." This is the administrator's or government's viewpoint which may create confusion. The government imposes a commodity tax which is an indirect tax in the expectation that it will be shifted. But if the producer is unable to shift the tax on to the sellers, it is a direct tax.

It is therefore, convenient and better to discard the administrator's viewpoint on the distinction between direct and indirect taxes and follow the economist's viewpoint as given by Dr. Dalton.

Accordingly, income tax, corporation tax, wealth tax, gift tax, death duties, expenditure tax etc. are direct taxes. On the other hand, excise duties, import and export duties, sales tax, entertainment tax, passenger tax, etc. are indirect taxes.[82]

2.14. Types of Taxes by Incidence

1. **Direct Taxes**: Direct taxes are taxes imposed on incomes, profits and wealth of individuals and companies and the incidence cannot be shifted forward or backward. Examples of direct taxes include: income tax, estate/death duty, gift tax, supper profits tax, land tax, poll/social service tax, property tax, inheritance tax, capital gains tax, capital levy, and surtax and corporation/company tax. The mentioned examples can be explained below:

   a. **Income Tax**: A tax levied on people whose income is above a certain level. Income tax enjoys wide support because income is a good indicator of an individual's ability to pay. However, income taxes are hard to administer because measuring income is often difficult. For example, some people receive part of their income 'in kind'–in the form of goods and services rather than in cash. If government taxes cash income but not payments 'in kind' then people can avoid taxation by taking a higher proportion of their income 'in kind'. For people with permanent jobs in companies and government offices, the tax is usually deducted from their salaries through Pay As You Earn (PAYE) arrangement.

   b. **Property Tax**: A property tax is a tax levied on an individual's wealth. The value of the person's assets, both financial assets (such as stocks and bonds) and real assets (such as houses and cars) is considered.

   c. **Estate/Death Duty**: When a person dies, the property

---

that he or she leaves behind to others may be subject to tax. An estate tax is a tax on the deceased person's property, which includes everything the person owned at the time of death for example: money, houses, stock, bonds, proceeds from insurance policies, and material possessions. Most governments levy estate taxes before the deceased person's property is given out to heirs. The major aim of such taxes is to redistribute incomes among the population.

d. **Inheritance Tax**: This is a tax levied on the value of the deceased person's estate after the estate is passed to heirs. The heirs of the deceased person's property pay the tax. Estate and inheritance taxes are sometimes collectively called death taxes.

e. **Gift Tax**: A gift tax is a tax levied on the transfer of property between living people. It is imposed on the person who receives the gift.

f. **Capital Levy**: A special tax levied on the rich to finance emergencies like wars, famine, floods, and earthquakes.

g. **Land Tax**: A tax on land normally intended to target the big land owners who at times rent it out to farmers/tenants. It is intended to reduce monopoly of land by a few landlords.

h. **Capital Gains Tax:** A capital gains tax is a tax levied on the profit realized upon the sale of a capital asset. In many cases, the amount of capital gain is treated as income and subject to tax.

i. **Super Profits Tax**: A tax levied on the abnormal profits of companies. The tax is based on the profits that a company has earned above a certain level.

j. **Surtax:** Tax on people with exceedingly high incomes.

k. **Poll Tax:** A poll tax is also called a per capita tax, or capitation tax. It is a tax imposed as a set amount per individual within a country. Poll taxes are administratively cheap because they are easy to compute and collect and difficult to cheat. Some countries adjust the taxes to reflect the income levels of the taxpayers and hence are called graduated tax. In South Sudan this tax is called social service tax and is part of local government taxes. It is tax imposed on an adult male at Payam/Boma level.

2. **Corporation Tax/Company Tax:** The corporation tax is a tax based on the profits of a company. The corporation income tax is one of the most controversial types of taxes. Although the law treats corporations as independent entities capable of paying tax, many economists urge that only real people such as the shareholders who own the corporations bear the tax burden. In addition, the tax leads to double taxation of corporate income. Income is taxed once when it is earned by the corporation, and is again taxed a second time when it is paid out to shareholders in the form of dividends. Thus, company income faces a higher tax burden than personal income.

2.15. Advantages of Direct Taxes

Direct taxes have the following advantages compared to other forms of taxes:

a. **Cheap to collect:** When the taxes are directly deducted from the peoples' income by the employer and remitted to the government, it becomes cheap. The government does not need to employ tax assessors and collectors since the company and government departments that employ the people do this work.

b. **Convenient to pay because they are spread over a long period**: Salary income earners have a defined amount deducted from their salaries per month as tax instead of paying the tax in lump sum; this makes it convenient for the taxpayer.

c. **Direct taxes are flexible and are easily increased or decreased**:This means that government can easily use direct taxes to influence the level of economic activity.Taxes can be increased and decreased at short notice to regulate the economy.

d. **Direct taxes are simple to understand**: Most direct taxes are simple to understand since it is a percentage of the taxpayers' income.

e. Most direct taxes are progressive since the rich people pay taxes at higher rate than the rates at which the poor people pay.This fits in well with the principle of equity and helps in reducing income inequalities.

f. **More certain in terms of revenue to be collected**: Unlike indirect taxes, the direct taxes are more certain and predictable in terms of the expected revenue per year. This is useful for government planning. Direct taxes are also certain to the tax payers. The tax payers are sure of the amounts and the time at which to pay the taxes. Unlike indirect taxes whose productivity is affected by changes in consumers' tastes and preferences, the revenue from direct taxes is relatively stable over a long period.

g. Those considered unable to pay like the old, sick and unemployed, young, students and prisoners are easily exempted from the tax.

h. Direct taxes do not directly affect commodity prices, there-
    fore, are not inflationary. Direct taxes cannot be directly shift-
    ed to commodity prices as easily as the indirect taxes. This
    means that the direct taxes cannot easily lead to inflation.
i. Direct taxes are very effective at redistributing national in-
    come among the population. They are useful tools of income
    redistribution.

2.16. Disadvantages of Direct Taxes

Though direct taxes have many advantages, they also have the
following disadvantages compared to other forms of taxes:

a. In the developing countries with high levels of unemploy-
    ment and a large subsistence sector, incomes are very low and
    so the revenue that is generated from direct taxes is always
    very low.
b. Costs of assessment and collection are high when the taxpay-
    ers are scattered in different locations. The tax assessors must
    go to the people to assess and collect the taxes hence raising
    the costs and making them less economical.
c. It is very difficult to measure the taxable capacity of the peo-
    ple to determine how much income tax they have to pay.
    This leads to either over taxation or under taxation.
d. Direct taxes negatively affect the rate of capital inflow be-
    cause foreign investors will be scared of the taxes.
e. Most direct taxes are collected by local chiefs and leaders
    who lack competence to assess and collect taxes.
f. Disincentive to work and entrepreneurship. Innovation and
    invention is discouraged, as people fear to undertake new
    projects for fear of paying additional taxes.
g. Direct taxes are very easy to evade. People can conceal their

incomes, others get income from other sources and yet others are not resident in a single place. This makes assessment and collection complicated making it easy for some people to evade the taxes.

h. Direct taxes inform of company profits hinder the expansion of firms since profits are taxed. The profits that would have been ploughed back into the firm for expansion are taken away in form of taxes and because the tax collectors usually target big companies, the small firms do not find incentives to expand as expansion means paying more taxes by them.

i. Narrow coverage and hence low revenue. Many people do not qualify to pay taxes due to low income and other considerations like old age, disability and unemployment.

j. Direct taxes are easily noticeable by the public and therefore can cause political and social resentment. Unlike the indirect taxes that are 'hidden', direct taxes breed unpopularity among the tax collectors and the government that imposes them.

k. Direct taxes on income discourage work as people would now prefer to enjoy more leisure than do more work that is taxed.

l. Direct taxes on company profits may be translated into lower wages and less benefits for workers. This has a big negative impact on the workers' standard of living, morale and output of the taxed firm.

m. High direct taxes scare away foreign experts from working within the country and also cause 'brain drain' of highly skilled and scarce labour-force.

2.17. Indirect Taxes

Indirect taxes are also called expenditure taxes or outlay taxes. Indirect taxes are taxes levied on expenditure; the tax is paid when a person/firm spends on commodities. These taxes are collected through producers or suppliers of the commodity. The tax incidence may rest on the producer or consumer of the commodity depending on the elasticity of demand and elasticity of supply of the commodity.

The following are some examples of indirect taxes. Customs duties, Excise duty, Sales tax/Turn over tax, Sumptuary tax, Octoroi tax and Value Added Tax.

a. **Customs duties**: An import or export duty is a tax levied on the movement of goods across a political border.

b. **Excise duty**: A tax on selected locally produced products whether the commodities are for local consumption or export. The goods and services liable to excise duty are cigarettes, beer, spirits, wines, soft drinks, airtime, cement, fuel, sugar.

c. **Sale tax/Turnover tax**: This is a tax on commodities sold within the country irrespective of whether the goods have been produced locally or imported.

d. **Sumptuary tax**: This is a prohibitive tax, on specific commodities to discourage their consumption e.g. tax on cigarettes whose purpose is to make them expensive and hence discourage smokers from buying them.

e. **Octoroi tax**: Tax on goods crossing or on transit through a country. A country charges Octoroi tax on goods passing through its territory going to other countries. For example, Uganda may charge Octoroi on goods passing through Ugandan territory to South Sudan.

f. Value Added Tax (VAT): Value added tax (VAT) is also known as 'Goods and Services Tax' (G.S.T), or turnover tax. VAT is a tax on the value added to a commodity at each stage of production. In the production of sweets for example, the farmer grows sugarcane and sells them to a sugar mill that then turns the sugarcane into sugar. The miller sells the sugar to a confectioner who makes sweets and sells them to consumers. At each stage, the producer adds value to the commodity.

VAT is usually administered by requiring the company to complete a VAT return form, giving details of the VAT it has been charged by its suppliers (referred to as input tax) and the VAT it has charged its customers (referred to as output tax). The difference between the output tax and input tax is the tax payable to the tax authority. If input tax is greater than output tax, the company can claim back money from the tax authority.

Because VAT is levied as a percentage of the value added to the commodity, it is an ad valorem tax. By collecting the tax at each production level, the theory is that the entire economy helps in the enforcement and collection of the tax. However, forged invoices and other similar evasive methods have demonstrated that there are always those who will attempt to evade taxation.

Economic theorists have argued that the collection process of VAT minimizes market distortions resulting from the tax, compared to sales tax. However, VAT is held by some school of thought that it discourages production.

2.17.1. Advantages of Indirect Tax

The advantages of indirect tax are as follows:

a. **Convenient**: Indirect taxes are convenient because they are paid when one has money to spend on the taxed commodities.

b. **Economical to collect**: Cheap to collect since they are collected through a few producers and sellers.

c. **Generate more revenue**: Indirect taxes generate more revenue for government compared to the direct taxes. The existence of indirect taxes therefore enables government to raise enough revenue to finance its expenditure. They can be made to cover wide variety of goods and services to maximize revenue collection.

d. **Indirect taxes direct consumption**: They are helpful in directing consumption behaviour of the population. They can be used to discourage the consumption of harmful goods. Consumption of such goods as tobacco and alcohol is discouraged by imposing high taxes on them.

e. **Encourage work**: Indirect taxes are less harmful to work as compared to direct taxes. An indirect tax increases the price of commodities and the worker must work more hours to be able to continue consuming the goods and services such a person was consuming before the tax.

f. **Protects domestic industries**: Indirect taxes protect domestic infant industries. By imposing taxes on imported goods, the country protects its own infant industries from excessive competition that would otherwise cause their collapse.

g. **Difficult to evade**: Indirect taxes are unavoidable and more difficult to evade. Since they are paid as purchases are made, they cannot be easily evaded.

h. **Flexible**: Indirect taxes are more flexible than direct taxes and are easily adjusted upwards or downwards to achieve desired goals according to changing economic conditions.

i. Unlike the direct taxes, indirect taxes are not easily noticed and therefore are less likely to cause political unrest.

2.17.2. Disadvantages of Indirect Taxes

The disadvantages of indirect taxes are as follows:

a. **Regressive**: They are regressive. They take from the rich and the poor the same amount and in the process, the poor spend a bigger percentage of their income on taxes than the rich.

b. **Inflationary**: Indirect taxes cause inflation by increasing transport costs, labour costs, and costs of raw materials. When placed on trade activities, indirect taxes directly increase the prices of goods and services. This causes cost-push inflation within the economy.

c. **Uncertain**: The revenue from indirect taxes is less certain and difficult to estimate. This makes planning difficult. Because the taxes are not compulsory, consumers and producers can decide to abandon the taxed commodity, in extreme cases, indirect taxes yield no or very little revenue especially if the rate is very high.

d. Another demerit of indirect taxes is that by discouraging demand through higher prices, they discourage production and investment. This has additional negative effects on employment and balance of payments of a country.

e. Indirect taxes interfere with consumers' sovereignty and divert production and consumption habits of people. People will not consume those goods and services they like but those on which less taxes are imposed because if their preferred choices have been highly taxed, they become unaffordable.

f. By causing an increment in the price of commodities, indirect taxes increase the cost of living and hence people are forced to go without some necessities and to consume poor quality goods, which decrease people's standard of living.

g. Indirect taxes discourage international trade. Taxes on locally produced commodities make them very expensive for foreign markets while import duties make imports too expensive for the local market. The result is a reduction in exports and or imports. This negatively affects the balance of payments of the country.

h. Misallocation of resources to non-taxed economic activities that may not be very relevant to the needs of the people and the country.

i. The producers may take advantage of the tax to increase prices more than the increase in tax and hence exploit the consumers.

2.18. Incidence of a Tax

Incidence of a tax is the final resting place of a tax (who finally pays the tax levied) depending on the elasticity of demand and supply of the taxed commodity.

The burden of a tax often lies elsewhere from where the tax is levied. One cannot tell the burden of a tax by looking at whom the tax is imposed on or what the tax is called. It is worthwhile to be clear about some terminologies related to this concept.

a. The statutory or formal incidence of a tax refers to the individual or a group that must legally pay the tax. It refers to the person or company on whom the tax is imposed and collected from. The person who pays the money for the tax.

b. Incidence of a tax or initial economic incidence shows the 'final resting place' of a tax depending on how demand and supply conditions for the taxed commodity allocate the tax between the producers and consumers of the commodity. A producer of a commodity can shift the tax imposed to consumers of the commodity inform of higher prices. If for example, milk producers raise the price of milk because of a tax, then the milk producers have shifted the milk tax to the consumers in form of higher prices and the incidence of the tax has fallen on the milk consumers.

c. Burden of a tax refers to changes in people's economic be-haviour in terms of consumption, savings and resource use because of a tax.

Take an example of a tax on sugar. The formal incidence falls on the manufacturer who pays the tax directly to the govern-ment. The incidence falls on the consumers in form of higher prices. The burden is felt in terms of reduced land exploitation, unemployment (workers laid off due to less demand that is caused by high post tax prices) etc. The burden of a tax is therefore seen in real terms not money terms.

The law establishes from whom a tax is supposed to be col-lected. For example, the law may specify that any person that manufactures beer pays a tax. However, who ultimately pays the tax (who bears the incidence) is determined by the market price as taxes spill over into production costs and hence into the prices of the commodities that consumers buy. For example, a tax on fuel may actually be paid by travelers in form of higher transport fares.

The key determinant of where the incidence of the tax falls is the price elasticity of demand and price elasticity of supply of the commodity being taxed. For example, where the incidence of the tax on fuel falls, will depend on the elasticity of demand, and the elasticity of supply for fuel.

Depending on the elasticity of demand and the elasticity of supply for the taxed commodity, the tax can be absorbed by the seller in the form of lower pre-tax costs, or by the buyer in form of higher post-tax prices or shared (not necessarily equally).

2.19. Relevance of the Concept of Tax Incidence

The theory of tax incidence has a number of practical applications:

1. Because businesses are more sensitive to wages than employees, payroll taxes, and other taxes collected from the employer end up being borne by the employee in form of reduced wages. The tax is passed onto the employee in the form of lower wages.

2. If the government requires employers to provide employees with health care, security fund contributions and other compulsory payments, the burden of this will fall almost entirely on the employee because the employer will pass on the burden in the form of lower wages.

3. Taxes on easily substitutable goods, such as beef and fish are mostly borne by the producer because the demand for easily substitutable goods is quite elastic.

4. The burden of tariffs (import taxes) for example taxes on imported commodities with elastic demand is borne entirely by the foreign producers.

5. The best sources of revenue are those commodities whose

demand is elastic since the producer can easily forward the tax to the consumer. Where demand is elastic and the producer cannot absorb all the taxes, he will stop production and the government does not get the tax because production has stopped.

2.20. Tax Evasion and Tax Avoidance

Tax evasion is failing to pay legally due taxes. One important way that high tax rates affect behaviour is by increasing evasion. For example, people may fail to report income to the government, thus reducing their tax bill and the government's tax revenue.

Tax avoidance occurs when people change their behaviour to reduce the amount of taxes they legally owe. When individuals relocate their business to a state with lower taxes or take advantage of loopholes in tax laws, they are practicing tax avoidance. There is nothing illegal about tax avoidance.

2.21. Reasons of Non-Compliance with Tax Laws

Noncompliance of tax laws is either intentional or unintentional failure of taxpayers to meet their tax obligations. This lack of compliance can be as a result of different factors as indicated below:

1. **A Rising or High Tax Burden**: Individuals and organizations tend to be noncompliant to tax laws when the taxes are deemed to be high as compared with the cost of living. In such a case taxpayers will tend to avoid payment of taxes so as to have a sizeable amount of money to be used in the purchase of different commodities.

2. **Lack of Knowledge on Tax Laws**: This point focuses on the unintentional failure of a taxpayer to comply with tax

laws. An example would be a small or medium enterprise that does not know that it is required by law for their businesses to be registered and as such pay taxes. Further, taxpayers would like the actual location or requirements needed for them to comply.

3. **Complexity of Tax Laws**: Unintentional non-compliance may also be caused by the complexity of tax laws, that is by the difficulty of keeping accurate records and the inability to obtain the information needed to comply. For example, low-income taxpayers who cannot afford to employ tax agents could face problems of understanding basic laws and even routine mathematical operations and interpreting the tax tables may present problems.

4. **Tax Evasion**: Tax evasion is the failure to declare taxable activity or income and this is a practice in the employment of the services such as consultancies, builders, plumbers and decorators. This intentional noncompliance requires the taxpayer to have some measure of understanding of the tax system.

5. **Weak Tax System**: This can also lead to intentional non-compliance of tax laws as taxpayers are able to utilize loopholes in the tax system. As such, this encourages taxpayers to be noncompliant as they are assured of not facing prosecution.

2.22. Distinction of Non-Tax Revenue of the Government

Non-tax revenue of the government is divided into three sections:[83]

1. **Currency, Coinage and Mint**: This category covers the

---

83   Bhatia. Op. cit. P. 36.

receipts of Currency Note Press, Security Paper Mill, and Bank Note Press and of the Mints. Profit from circulation of small coins is also included here.

2. **Interest Receipts, Dividends and Profits**: This section comprises of interest receipts on loans by the government to other parties, dividends and profits from public sector undertakings run by or as government departments including other income generating departments.

3. **Other Non-Tax Revenue**: This section covers revenue from various government activities and services such as from administrative services, public service commission, police, jails, agriculture and allied services, industry and minerals, water and power development services, transport and communications, supplies and disposal, public works, education, housing, information and publicity, broadcasting, grants-in-aid and contributions etc. Income and profit from the creation of currency by the government, i.e., the excess of face value of currency over its cost of creation are also included in this group of revenue.

2.23. Buoyancy

Buoyancy is the term that highlights the reasons for an increase in the yield of a tax over time. An increase in tax revenue on account of a growth of its base is termed as its buoyancy. A buoyant tax has an inherent tendency to yield more tax revenue with the growth of its base. Thus, for example, with given rates of income tax and the definition of taxable income, if yield from income tax increases as national income increases, it would be termed a buoyant tax. Similarly, excise duties are levied on production of specified goods. If new items are not brought under these duties and the rates of existing duties remain unchanged, but the revenue from excise duties still increases with an increase in the production of excisable items, we have a case of buoyancy of excise duties. It is clear that the concept of buoyancy may be applied to an individual tax or to a whole set of taxes. Numerically, the buoyancy of a tax is measured as a ratio of the proportionate increase in tax revenue to a proportionate increase in the tax base.[84]

2.24. Elasticity of a Tax

Elasticity of a tax is also another term that highlights the reasons for an increase in the yield of a tax over time. The yield of a tax may also go up on account of extension of its coverage or a revision of its rates. Such a characteristic of a tax is referred to as its elasticity. In other words, elasticity of a tax refers to its responsiveness to steps taken by authorities in increasing its yield through an extension of its coverage or revision of its rates. Numerically, the elasticity of a tax is measured by the ratio of proportionate change in its yield to the proportionate change in its coverage or rates.[85]

2.25. Tax Heavens

International rules on global tax system…do not directly authorize tax abuse. Instead, either by design or by accident, they create spaces for potential abuse. Since 1960s in particular, this space has been filled by an ever more complex network of offshore financial centres (OFCs) more popularly known as 'tax heavens' or 'secrecy jurisdictions' designed in large part to facilitate secrecy, tax avoidance and tax evasion. These are legal jurisdictions offering a combination of low tax rates for foreign individual

---

84   Ibid. p. 40.

85   Ibid. p. 40.

companies, limited regulation, and extreme secrecy about the ownership of registered corporations and individual assets. This secrecy has been achieved, among other things, through national bank secrecy laws designed to prevent the sharing of information about clients, even with national authorities, and by making it easy to register 'shell corporations' that is, legal corporations that have few or no substantive activities in the country. These policies are designed to attract 'offshore'—that is, foreign wealth and corporations by disguising the identities of their owners, and by moving them beyond the reach of national authorities.[86]

This in turn, has been a fundamentally beggar-thy-neighbour strategy. Financial service providers within secrecy jurisdictions achieve economic gain by offering services to foreign capital, but to do so by undermining tax laws elsewhere in the world. From a societal perspective, the costs certainly outweigh the comparatively modest economic benefits to tax heavens themselves. While the term 'tax heaven' generally evokes images of small Caribbean islands, there is a growing recognition that this is misleading. If the focus is on countries that employ secrecy and idiosyncratic benefits to attract foreign companies and wealth, the primary culprits are, in fact, members of the OECD. The largest recipient of offshore financial wealth remains Switzerland, with London, New York, Luxembourg, Singapore and others close behind. Meanwhile, research by Findley, Nielson and Sharman (2014) has found that the easiest place globally to create a secretive corporate entity is the US State of Delaware.[87]

---

86   Mick Moore, Wilson Prichard and Odd-Helge F. Jeldstad. Op. Cit. P. 42.

87   Ibid. Pp. 42-43.

2.26. Complexity and Loopholes of Tax Heavens

While the network of tax heavens has provided the infrastructure for international tax abuse, that abuse has thrived on the complexity of the global tax system. Notwithstanding a bias in favour of wealthier countries, international tax rules are, for the most part, formally intended to ensure that individuals and corporations pay appropriate taxes in the jurisdictions where they live and operate. However, the complexity and imperfections of those rules have created scope for lawyers, accountants and advisors to find loopholes through which their wealthy individual and corporate clients are able to minimize their tax payments. While tax heavens have provided a destination for individuals and MNCs seeking to avoid taxation, complexity, grey areas and loopholes have provided the facilitation environment that has allowed funds to flow into tax heavens. Unsurprisingly, then, when efforts have been made to reform the international tax system, calls for simplification have often been met with fierce resistance by those who benefit from existing arrangements.[88]

Collectively, these features of international tax system pose challenges for all countries. However, these challenges are particularly acute for governments of low income countries. They have had little to say in developing the rules. The complexity of those rules means that national tax agencies require highly specialized accountancy and legal skills if they are to fight their corner. But these skills are in limited supply everywhere-and particularly in most African states. Multinational firms and wealthy individuals supported by transnational accounting and professional services firms-typically employ teams of lawyers and accountants that are larger and much better paid than those working in nation-

---

88   Ibid. p. 43.

al tax agencies. Against this background, we can now look at the challenge in more detail, focusing first on tax avoidance by wealthy individuals, and then on equivalent efforts by MNCs.[89]

2.27. International Tax Rules benefit High Net Worth Individuals

Although the tax activities of MNCs have received the most critical publicity in recent years, there is mounting evidence that tax losses arising from tax avoidance and evasion by wealthy individuals may be a similar size. The key actors are so-called high net worth individuals (HNWIs): individuals with at least $1 million in financial wealth. While few in number, they control a large and growing share of national income in most countries. According to the Global Wealth Report (Credit Suisse 2017), there are 36.1 million millionaires in the world, making up 0.7% of world adults and accounting for a total of $128.7 trillion, or 45.9% of the world's wealth. While this share is rising significantly faster in Africa than in any other region in the world (Bird 2015). Of the twenty countries whose ultra-wealthy ($30 million or more in net assets) populations are estimated to have grown most rapidly over the last decade, 11 are in Africa (Knight Frank Research 2017). All told, one recent estimate is that there are 145,000 HNWIs in Africa, who control about $800 million of total wealth (New World Wealth 2017)-though even this is likely an under estimate, owing to the large proportion of wealth offshore (Zucman 2014).

It is difficult to tax HNWIs because of the following:

1. they are mobile internationally;
2. much of their income is in the form of capital gains on investments;

---

89   Ibid. pp. 43-44.

3. they can employ expensive advisers to assist them in developing complex tax avoidance strategies;
4. they often have influence with and cooperation from political elites (Fjeld-stad and Heggstad 2014).

Unsurprisingly, there are indications that efforts by HNWIs to avoid taxes have accelerated with the spread of globalization. Recent studies in South Africa, Kenya and Uganda have suggested that the lists of HNWIs held by tax authorities may capture fewer than 10% of those they should (Forslund 2012; Kumar 2014;kangave et al.2016).

Perhaps the most revealing illustration of the magnitude and brazenness of tax evasion and avoidance by HNWIs came in early 2015, when a list of clients of HSBC bank with secret accounts in Switzerland became public. The leaked documents revealed that, in 2007, and in just one bank in one country, people resident in Sub-Sahara Africa held over $6.5 billion in secret accounts. This accorded with earlier stories of powerful Africans with vast and mostly illicit wealth held overseas. Perhaps the most famous is the case of Sani Abacha, who is estimated to have stolen $2 and $5 billion, and possibly more, during his five years as president of Nigeria (Barry 2015). These and similar stories are a reminder that this is not merely a story about tax evasions, but also about the ways in which secrecy in the international system reinforces inequality, facilitates political corruption, and undermines democracy.[90]

---

90   Ibid. pp. 45.

2.28. Effective Tax Policy for a Developing Country

A developing country must have a different tax policy from a developed country, because:

1. Its primary objective is to achieve high level of economic development, not merely economic stability.
2. Greater attention has to be paid to the maximization of revenue and not ability to pay or equity.
3. It has to follow a policy of active intervention in economic affairs and not laissez-faire.
4. It aims at accelerating economic growth and not to reduce economic inequalities.

A developing country must aim at raising the rate of saving by taxing the big industrialists and landlords and divert consumption to productive enterprises. The tax policy must mobilize economic surpluses, i.e. excess of current output over essential consumption, for accelerating economic growth. In underdeveloped countries, greater attention needs to be paid to indirect taxes, because:

1. They promote development by checking conspicuous consumption.
2. Mobilize resources for the public sector.
3. Increase the saving ration.[91]

The aims of a suitable tax policy for the underdeveloped countries must be:

1. To divert resources from private to public sector.
2. From consumption goods industries to investment goods industries.
3. From import goods to export goods.

---

91   Saleemi. Op. cit. p. 36.

2.29. Failure of Tax Systems in Africa

Concerns about fairness, equity and reciprocity are thus pervasive among taxpayers. Yet popular initiatives to improve tax systems have been rare, both in Sierra Leon and elsewhere. This seems to reflect a broad sense among taxpayers that the failures of national and local tax systems are firmly rooted in the realities of power[92] and politics. It is commonly believed that powerful individuals do not pay taxes that they owe-be they income taxes, corporate taxes, trade taxes, property taxes or others-because of the political influence they enjoy. Official data almost everywhere seems to confirm this story. While taxation is often presented as a highly specialist, technical and rule-bound enterprise, taxpayers themselves often have a visceral sense that politics explains much of what occurs in practice.[93]

Currently in Africa and among its aid donors, there is much emphasis on increasing total tax collection, with frequent suggestions that governments should aim to collect no less than 15% of gross domestic product (GDP) in taxes-and, in some cases, suggestion of targets as high as 20%. This is argued to be the minimum needed to finance public goods and service-sometimes equated with achieving the UN's Sustainable Development Goals. However, the use of such targets has prompted an important objection: expanded revenue collection is worthwhile only if that revenue is translated efficiently into valuable public goods and services. Yet we know that this often does not happen, and the use of revenue targets could, at worse, motivate and validate more coercive forms of tax collection.[94]

---

92   Mick Moore, Wilson Prichard and Odd-Helge F. Jeldstad. Op. Cit. P. 4.

93   Ibid. p. 5.

94   Ibid. p. 12.

Arguments in favour of the expansion of taxation are often linked to the belief in the potential of such an expansion to contribute to state-building and increased government account-ability. A particular narrative about these links has become rela-tively widespread in recent years. This narrative holds that states that rely heavily on taxation to fund their activities-as opposed to relying on natural resource wealth or foreign aid-are more likely to build a strong state structures and become accountable to their taxpayer citizens. A government seeking to collect its own tax revenue will be forced to build more effective pub-lic sector organizations to collect that revenue; this will include, for example, a wider use of meritocratic hiring and promotion practices, improved business and land registries, stronger law en-forcement and judiciaries. Meanwhile, the expansion of taxation may prompt processes of 'tax bargaining' and the construction of new 'fiscal social contracts' as taxpayers resist taxation, make demands for reciprocity and enter into constructive interaction with governments. This narrative is grounded in the history of taxation and state-building in early modern Europe, but appears to be supported by the results of recent research in Africa and elsewhere in developing world.

However, while the casual links set out in the narrative are potentially powerful, they are also seductive and can easily be over-simplified and robbed of necessary nuance, complexi-ty and local content. There is clear evidence that taxation can be, and has been, a driver of expanded political responsiveness and accountability, and a spur to constructing new state capac-ity. However, it is equally clear that these positive connections are not guaranteed. Taxation is everywhere, in large part an ex-ercise in the use of coercive power, as states extract resources from citizens. Whether the process leads to state-building and accountability depends on the broader characteristics of the state doing the taxing, the nature of political resources possessed by taxpayers, and the characteristics of tax systems themselves. The big questions are thus not about whether taxation can in principle be a spur to improved state-citizen relations and accountability, but about when and how such connections are likely, and how these positive processes might be supported.[95]

2.30. Effect of Unfair International Tax Rules on Development in Africa

On 25th March 2014, people in Abuja, Nigeria witnessed a surprising scene: a public protest, outside a meeting of the African Union finance ministers, to highlight unfair international tax rules that were holding black African development. Why would anyone bother to try to ignite public debate about such a dull, remote and technical issue? While protests against taxes are not unusual, the demonstrators were calling for more taxes-on transnational companies. The subject might be complex, but the core of their argument was straight forward: international tax rules have allowed wealthy individuals and multinational enterprises, aided and abetted by global tax heavens and the accountants and lawyers that support them, to evade and avoid their obligations to the societies from where they draw their incomes and profits. Cracking down these abuses would help finance development and combat inequality and corruption.[96]

In South Africa, as in many other countries, the narrative of large-scale international tax evasion, facilitated by the abuse of

---

95   Ibid. p. 13.
96   Ibid. p. 37.

power by internationally connected elites, shapes popular understandings of the causes of growing inequality. This emerging 'tax justice' movement argues that unfair international tax rules have undermined the public finances of lower-income countries by facilitating tax evasion and avoidance by wealthy companies and individuals. Existing international tax rules have created, either by accident or by design, a system characterized by extensive secrecy, excessive complexity and widespread loopholes. It is increasingly difficult for national tax authorities to tax mobile wealth. The most striking manifestation of this system has been the growth of a global system of offshore financial centres better known as 'tax heavens' or 'secrecy jurisdictions'-which have offered a destination for both wealthy individuals and multinational corporations (MNCs) seeking to minimize their tax payments and disguise their wealth. While most governments find that their potential revenues are being hijacked in this way, the outflows are especially high from Africa and other low-income regions: there is limited capacity to implement effectively the complex rules and procedures that might stem the revenue leakages.[97]

Tax evasion and avoidance by MNCs and wealthy individuals have seriously dented tax revenue in Africa. As we explain… we do not know the precise size of the tax losses-except that they are big. But tax evasion and avoidance do wider damage. International tax rules have not offered opportunities for evasion and avoidance equally, but have almost exclusively benefited wealthy individuals and MNCs. They have thus contributed to reinforcing and deepening existing inequality, potentially distorting economic competition in favour of international companies,

---

97   Ibid. p. 38.

and creating downward pressure on the rates at which governments can levy taxes on wealthy individuals and transnational
corporations. The same rules have generated new opportunities
for corruption, through the complex structures of transnational enterprises, tax heavens, secret bank accounts, and secretive
legal managements to obscure the real ownership of assets.[98]

2.31. Challenges to Low-Income Countries in the International Arena

The basic challenges faced by governments of low-income
countries in the international arena are little different from those
facing tax collectors anywhere. Governments are keen to tax the
profits of corporations and the earnings of wealthy individuals
according to the national laws, while many of these potential
taxpayers aim to disguise and hide as much profit and wealth
as possible. The challenges of taxing economic transactions are
distinct because of the complexity of the global tax system. In a
world in which capital (money) can flow freely across national
borders, wealthy individuals and multinational companies have
many opportunities to disguise and hide their wealth from national governments. In principle, effective international cooperation could overcome these challenges. In practice, cooperation
has been limited. In strict sense of the term, there is no international tax system. There is rather a network of (overlapping)
national arrangements; bilateral treaties; principles endorsed by
international organizations, above all Organization for Economic Cooperation and Development (OECD), international agreements; and custom and practice. Some of the resultant 'rules' are
soft, implicit and contested; others are firmer and legally bind-

---

98   Ibid. p. 39.

ing. Their effectiveness depends largely on willing compliance. Among the actors with power to enforce compliance, the government of the United States is most prominent. There is no global tax organization-not even one with limited powers like the World Trade Organization (WTO). The international tax system has come to be characterized by unequal decision-making power, escalating complexity and the emergence of growing secrecy, with potentially serious development consequences.[99]

---

99   Ibid. p. 40.

Chapter Three

PUBLIC FINANCE

3.1. Introduction

In economics, the word 'public' is generally used to refer to what belongs to or what is related to the country or a community as a whole. Because governments are charged with managing resources on behalf of all the people, 'public' will, in the many times we come across it refer to activities related to government.[100]

Public finance is defined as the science that deals with the study of government revenue and expenditure. Public finance is made up of the branches of: public revenue, public expenditure,

---

100   Mutamba. Op. cit. p. 240.

public debt, fiscal policy and financial administration.[101]

Before a more detailed study of public finance is done, we need to understand and get a general background of the importance of government in an economy. The major aim of governments in economic activities and interventions is to improve the welfare of the people and to ensure economic stability. Government intervenes in economic activities and regulates the activities of the private sector mainly to achieve these objectives.[102]

The level of government intervention in economic activities differs depending on the type of economic system. The way government intervenes in a socialist economic system differs from the way it intervenes in a capitalist system.

Government intervenes in an economy in any of the following ways:[103]

1. Regulating the activities of the private sector to ensure proper use of national resources and protect consumers from exploitation.

2. Establishing laws and enforcing them to ensure an orderly business environment.

3. Producing goods and services especially those which the private sector may not properly or adequately produce and supply.

4. Reducing income inequalities among individuals, sectors and regions of the economy.

5. Stabilizing the economy through the use of monetary and fiscal policies so as to regulate prices, unemployment, foreign trade and etc.

---

101   Ibid. p.240.

102   Ibid. p. 240.

103   Ibid. pp. 240–241.

6. Imposing taxes and providing grants and subsidies for purchase of goods and services from the private sector to encourage or discourage certain activities and products.

7. Providing and maintaining infrastructure in form of hospitals, schools, roads, dams and telecommunications.

8. These are some of the ways in which the government intervenes in economic activities and influences what individuals, firms and other players that make decisions.

3.2. Public Revenue

Public revenue means the income of the government from taxes, prices, special assessments and state enterprises. It means those amounts which are received by the government from different sources. In other words, the income of government is known as public revenue.[104]

Like any other economic unit, a government needs funds to finance its activities. Such funds are raised from various sources.[105] The important sources of revenue include "taxes, income from currency, market borrowings, sale of public assets, and income from public undertakings, fees, fines, gifts and donations."[106]

Public revenue is money collected by government for the common good of the country. The government on behalf of its people finances common services and goods in form of education, security, health, pensions and administration of the country. There are many and varied sources from which government raise revenue to finance these activities.

Some of the sources of public revenue are internal and others

---

104   Saleemi. Op. cit. P. 2.

105   Bhatia. Op. cit. P. 35.

106   Ibid. p. 35.

are external. Others are short term while others are long term. The main sources of public revenue are:[107]

1. **Taxes**: A tax is a legal compulsory levy that individuals and private companies are required to pay to the government based on their incomes or the nature of their activities. A tax is also defined as a compulsory contribution collected by the government for public use. A tax is not a value for value payment. It is a non quid pro quo payment. This means that no goods or services are directly exchanged for the amount of tax. Taxes are direct or indirect. Examples of taxes are income tax, corporation tax, and import tax, value added tax etc.

    Tax is the most important source of public revenue. Tax may be defined as the compulsory contribution imposed on the individuals to meet the expenses which are incurred for a common cause.[108]

    Taxes may be of different kinds e.g.:

    a. Income Tax: This tax is imposed on the incomes of individuals.
    b. Corporation Tax: This tax is imposed on profits of limited companies.
    c. Sales tax: This tax is imposed on the sale of commodities.
    d. Excise tax: This tax is imposed on the production of commodities.
    e. Custom Duty: This tax is imposed on the import or export of commodities.[109]

2. **Fees**: A fee is money paid in direct exchange for professional services rendered. Government provide certain services and

---

107   Mutamba. Op. cit. pp. 241-242.

108   Saleemi. Op. cit. p. 2.

109   Ibid. p. 2.

charges fees. For example, fees are paid to government for such services as education in public schools and universities, land surveying, use of public libraries, weigh bridges, and company registration. A fee is paid for a specific service directly provided to the person paying it.[110]

Fee is that amount which is received by the government against any direct services rendered by the government e.g. road license fee, import license fee etc.[111]

3. **Fines and Penalties**: Government raises revenue from fines and penalties imposed on people who commit crimes or break the law. Traffic offences are a common example on which fines are paid.[112]

If the individuals do not obey the laws of the country then the fines are imposed on such individuals. These fines are also the income of the government.[113]

4. **Prices**: Prices are those amounts which are received by the government for commercial services e.g. railway fare, postage and telephone charges etc.[114]

5. **Special Assessments**: Special assessments are those amounts which are charged for specific purposes. For example, if the government charges a specific amount from the residents of a particular area for the establishment of a secondary school in that area then it will be a special assessment.[115]

6. **State Property**: The forests, mines and national parks are

---

110   Mutamba. Op. cit. p. 241-242.

111   Saleemi. Op. cit. p. 2

112   Mutamba. Op. cit. pp. 241-242.

113   Saleemi. Op. cit. p. 2.

114   Ibid. p. 2.

115   Ibid. p. 2.

considered as the government property. The income from such departments is also one source of public revenue.[116]

7. **Grants**: These are financial donations given to the government to cater for the costs of specific projects or to help a country out of a specific financial dilemma.

8. **Deficit Financing**: This is where the government orders the printing and minting of more currency notes and coins to finance its expenditure. It also involves the central government borrowing from the central bank as a means of getting revenue for its expenditure.

9. **Loans**: The government raises revenue by borrowing internally or externally. External loans are got from other countries, multinational financial institutions like the International Monetary Fund (IMF), World Bank, and International Development Agency (IDA) and also from foreign private banks. Internal loans are obtained from local commercial banks, development banks, mutual funds, insurance companies and individuals.

10. **Profits from Business Activities**: The government at times owns companies or shares in public companies. From such companies, the government gets profits as revenue. Current economic trends emphasize government pulling itself from business activities through privatization and as such, revenue from this source is reducing in most countries.

11. **Securities:** Government may raise money by issuing securities such as treasury bills and bonds. By issuing securities, the government is able to get money which it pays back to the security holders when the securities mature.

12. **Licenses**: A license is a document that authorizes a person

---

116   Ibid. p. 3.

or company to conduct business, own something or deal in a profitable activity. For example, the government will charge money for a license to fish from a river, to own a gun or operate a school or a clinic. This earns revenue to the government.

13. **Gambling**: Government raises revenue through gambling activities usually in form of lotteries e.g. National Lottery, etc.

14. **Other Sources of Government Revenue**: Different governments devise different methods to raise revenue in addition to the common ones mentioned above. Other sources include rent from property within and outside the country, public fund-raisings and sale of government property.

3.3. Government Receipts

It is a normal practice with a government to divide its receipts into "revenue" and "capital" categories. Broadly speaking, revenue receipts include "routine" and "earned" ones. Revenue receipts do not include borrowings and recovery of loans from other parties, but they do include tax receipts, donations, grants, fees, and fines etc. Capital receipts, on the other hand, cover those items which are basically of non-repetitive and non-routine variety and change government's financial liabilities/assets.[117]

3.4. Division of Tax Revenue

Tax revenue is divided into three sections:[118]

1. **Taxes on Income and Expenditure**: They cover all those taxes which are levied on receipts of income and expenditure

---

117   Ibid. p. 35.

118   Bhatia. Op. cit. pp. 35-36.

such as corporation tax, income tax, expenditure tax, and similar other taxes, if any, in force.

2. **Taxes on Property and Capital Transactions**: They cover taxes on specific forms of wealth and its transfers such as estate duty, wealth tax, gift tax, house tax, land revenue and stamps and registration fees, etc.

3. **Taxes on Commodities and Services**: They include taxes on production, sale, purchase, transport, storage, and consumption of goods and services.

3.5. Functions of the Government

The government performs the following functions:

1. **Protection Functions**: The government is responsible for maintaining peace and security in the country and to defend the country against external aggression. For this purpose, the government maintains police and armed forces.

2. **Administrative Functions**: The government is responsible for the administration of the country. Various administrative departments are established by the government for this purpose.

3. **Social Functions**: The government provides social services like education, health, housing etc. These services are vital for the welfare of the society.

4. **Development Functions**: The development of different sections of the economy is not possible without the state help. The government should develop irrigation, transport and communication, industrial and agricultural systems of the country for the rapid increase in the rate of economic growth.

In order to perform these functions effectively and adequately, the government needs funds. Taxation is an important source of the government income. The income of the government from taxes and other sources is known as public revenue.[119]

3.6. Public Expenditure

Public expenditure is spending made by the government of a country on collective needs and wants such as pension, provision, infrastructure, etc.[120] Until the 19th century, public expenditure was limited as laissez faire philosophies believed that money left in private hands could bring better returns.

Public expenditure refers to government expenditure. It is incurred by central, state and local governments. The public expenditure is incurred on various activities for the welfare of the people and also for the economic development, especially in developing countries. In other words, the expenditure incurred by public authorities like central, state and local governments to satisfy the collective social wants of the people is known as public expenditure.

Public expenditure or government expenditure is spending made by the central government and local/regional governments or state governments and includes loans and grants given out. It is any money that goes out of government coffers. Government expenditure arises out of the following:[121]

1. Recurrent expenditure (operating expenditure/cost) is incurred by government for the day to day running of the

---

119   Saleemi. Op. cit. Pp. 1-2.

120   Akrani, Gaurav. "Meaning of Public Expenditure". Retrieved 15 February 2012.

121   Saleemi. Op. cit. p. 264.

state and providing public services. Examples of recurrent expenditure include salaries to civil servants, fuel, drugs for government hospitals etc.

2. Capital expenditure (Development expenditure) is money spent on infrastructure, agriculture, buildings, hospitals etc. It is expenditure that increases the country's capital stock. For example, expenditures on building new roads, bridges, schools etc.

3. Transfer payments are transfers from tax-payers to benefit re-cipients through the working of the social security system. Transfer payments are non-quid-pro-quo payments because the recipients do not have to supply goods or services to re-ceive them. They include pensions, subsidies, relief supplies, bursaries etc.

4. Debt Interest: Expenditure on servicing government debts.

3.7. Need for Government Expenditure

Different governments have different spending policies. These policies change. Generally, we can identify the major objectives of government expenditure,[122] which are:

1. **Providing Public and Merit Goods**: Public goods can only be paid for by the state because individuals cannot pro-vide them since they cannot exclude non-payers from en-joying them.

2. **Redistribution of Income and Wealth**: The major aim of government expenditure is to redistribute income and to reduce income inequalities by providing a basic minimum level of income for the unemployed, old, disabled, and other low-income groups.

---

122   Ibid. pp. 264–265.

3. **Influencing Resource Allocation**: This is achieved through regional or sector policies which aim at reducing regional or sectorial economic imbalances. The government may provide grants and subsidies to selected sectors, firms, regions or service providers so as to influence their performance.

4. **Influencing the Level of Macro Economic Activity**: Public spending plays a big role in stabilizing the level of aggregate demand in the economy. Increase in government expenditure can have multiplier effects on the final level of national income.

5. **Regulating Economic Activities**: The major function of government is to regulate the activities of the private sector to ensure the safety, health and welfare of the public. Standards must be set and enforced. For example, Standards of Bureau of South Sudan must ensure that customers are not cheated. Government must spend on enforcing law and order to achieve the above.

As noted earlier, level of government spending changes. It is influenced by or depends on the following:

1. Political views.
2. Rate of interest.
3. Inflation rate.
4. Changes in population size and structure (demographics).
5. Changes in economic activity. For example, reducing production and unemployment demands for more expenditure on social benefits for the unemployed.
6. Demand for merit goods like education and health services.
7. Changes in technology.
8. Natural factors like bad weather, floods, epidemics etc.
9. Political stability and conflicts.

3.8. Objectives of Public Expenditure

The major objectives of public expenditure are:

1. Administration of law and order and justice.
2. Maintenance of police force.
3. Maintenance of army and provision for defense goods.
4. Maintenance of diplomats in foreign countries.
5. Public Administration.
6. Servicing of public debt.
7. Development of industries.
8. Development of transport and communication.
9. Provision for public health.
10. Creation of social goods.

3.9. Types of Public Expenditure

Classification of public expenditure refers to the systematic arrangement of different items on which the government incurs expenditure. Public expenditure can be classified as follows:

1. **Capital and Revenue Expenditure:** Capital Expenditure of the government refers to that expenditure which results in creation of fixed assets. They are in the form of investment. They add to the net productive assets of the economy. Capital Expenditure is also known as development expenditure as it increases the productive capacity of the economy. It is investment expenditure and a non-recurring type of expenditure. For e.g. expenditure on agricultural and industrial development, irrigation dams, public enterprises etc., are all capital expenditures

   Revenue expenditures are current or consumption expenditures incurred on civil administration, defense forces, public health and, education, maintenance of government machinery etc. This type of "expenditure is of recurrent type which is incurred year after year.

2. **Development and Non–Developmental Expenditure/ Productive and Non–Productive Expenditure:** Expenditure on infrastructure development, public enterprises or development of agriculture increase productive capacity in the economy and bring income to the government. Thus they are classified as productive expenditure. All expenditures that promote economic growth development are termed as development expenditure.

    Unproductive (non – development) expenditure refers to those expenditures which do not yield any income. Expenditure such as interest payments, expenditure on law and order, public administration, do not create any productive asset which brings income to government such expenses are classified as unproductive expenditures.

3. **Transfer and Non-Transfer Expenditure:** Transfer expenditure refers to those kind of expenditures against which there is no corresponding transfer of real resources i.e., goods or services. Such expenditure includes public expenditure on: national old pension scheme, interest payments, subsidies, unemployment allowances, welfare benefits to weaker sections etc. By incurring such expenditure, the government does not get anything in return, but it adds to the welfare of the people, especially to weaker sections of society. Such expenditure results in redistribution of money incomes within the society.

    The non-transfer expenditure relates to that expenditure which results in creation of income or output. The non-transfer expenditure includes development as well as non-development expenditure that results in creation of output directly or indirectly, and covers: economic infrastructure (power, transport, irrigation etc.), social infrastructure (education, health and family welfare), internal law and order and defense, public administration etc. By incurring such expenditure, government creates a healthy environment for economic activities.

4. **Planned and Non–Planned Expenditure:** The plan expenditure is incurred on development activities outlined in ongoing five year plan. In 2009-10, the plan expenditure of Central Government was 5.3% of GDP. Planned expenditure is incurred on transport, rural development, communication, agriculture, energy, social services, etc.

The non-planned expenditure is incurred on those activities, which are not included in the five-year plan. It includes development and non-development expenditure. It includes: defense, subsidies, interest payments, maintenance etc.

5. **Other Classification:** Mrs. Hicks classified Public Expenditure on the basis of duties of government. It is as follows:

   a. **Defense Expenditure:** It is expenditure on defense equipment, wages and salaries of armed forces, navy and air-force etc. It is incurred by government to provide security to citizens of country from external aggression.

   b. **Civil Expenditure:** Government incurs this expenditure to maintain law and order and administration of justice.

   c. **Development Expenditure:** It is expenditure on development of agriculture, industry, trade and commerce, transport and communication etc.

3.10. Role of Public Expenditure in Promotion of Economic Development

In modern economic activities public expenditure has to play an important role. It helps to accelerate economic growth and ensure economic stability. Public Expenditure can promote economic development as follows:

1. To promote rapid economic development.
2. To promote trade and commerce.
3. To promote rural development
4. To promote balanced regional growth
5. To develop agricultural and industrial sectors
6. To build socio-economic overheads e.g. roadways, railways, power etc.
7. To exploit and develop mineral resources like coal and oil.
8. To provide collective wants and maximize social welfare.
9. To promote full employment and maintain price stability.
10. To ensure an equitable distribution of income.

3.11. Principles of Public Expenditure

The main principles or canons of public expenditure are as follows:

1. **The Principle of Maximum Social Advantage:** The government expenditure should be incurred in such a way that it should give benefit to the community as a whole. The aim of the public expenditure is the provision of maximum social advantage. If one section of the society or one particular group receives benefit of the public expenditure at the expense of the society as a whole, then that expenditure cannot be justified in any way, because it does not result in the greatest good to the public in general. So we can say that

the public expenditure should secure the maximum social advantage.

2. **The Principle of Economy:** The principle of economy requires that government should spend money in such a manner that all wasteful expenditure is avoided. Economy does not mean miserliness or niggardliness. By economy we mean that public expenditure should be increased without any extravagance and duplication. If the hard earned money of the people, collected through taxes, is thoughtlessly spent, the public expenditure will not conform to the cannon of economy.

3. **The Principle of Sanction:** According to the principle, all public expenditure should be incurred by getting prior sanction from the competent authority. The sanction is necessary because it helps in avoiding waste, extravagance, and overlapping of public money. Moreover, prior approval of the public expenditure makes it easy for the audit department to scrutinize the different items of expenditure and see whether the money has not been overspent or misappropriated.

4. **The Principle of Balanced Budgets:** Every government must try to keep its budgets well balanced. There should be neither ever recurring surpluses nor deficits in the budgets. Ever recurring surpluses are not desired because it shows that people are unnecessarily heavily taxed. If expenditure exceeds revenue every year, then that too is not a healthy sign because this is considered to be the sign of financial weakness of the country. The government, therefore, must try to live within its own means.

5. **The Principle of Elasticity:** The principle of elasticity requires that public expenditure should not in any way be

rigidly fixed for all times. It should be rather fairly elastic. The public authorities should be in a position to vary the expenditure as the situation demands. During the period of depression, it should be possible for the government to increase the expenditure so that economy is lifted from low level of employment. During boom period, the state should be in a position to curtail the expenditure without causing any distress to the people.

6. **No Unhealthy Effect on Production and Distribution:** The public expenditure should be arranged in such a way that it should not have adverse effect on production or distribution of wealth in the country. Public expenditure should aim at stimulating production and reducing inequalities of wealth distribution. If due to unwise public spending, wealth gets concentrated in a few hands, then its purpose is not served. The money really goes waste then.

3.12. Causes of Growth of Public Expenditure

There are several factors that have led to enormous increase in public expenditure through the years:

1. Defense expenditure due to modernization of defense equipment by navy, army and air force to prepare the country for war or for prevention causes-for-growth-of-public-expenditure.

2. **Population Growth**: It increases with the increase in population, more of investment is required to be done by government on law and order, education, infrastructure, etc. investment in different fields depending on the different age group is required.

3. **Welfare Activities**: Include the following:

a. Welfare, mid-day meals, pension provisions etc.

b. Provision of public and utility services-provision of basic public goods given by government (their maintenance and installation) such as transportation.

c. Accelerating economic growth-in order to raise the standard of living of the people.

d. Price rise: higher price level compels government to spend increased amount on purchase of goods and services.[123]

e. Increase in public revenue: with rise in public revenue government is bound to increase the public expenditure.

f. International obligation: maintenance of socio economic obligation, cultural exchange etc. (these are indirect expenses of government).

4. **Wars and Social Crises**: fighting amongst people and communities, and prolonged drought or unemployment, earthquake, hurricanes or tornadoes may lead to increase in public expenditure of a country. This is because it will involve governments to re-plan and allocate resources to finance the reconstruction.

5. Creation of super national organizations—e.g., the United Nations, North Atlantic Treaty Organization (NATO), European Community (EU) and other multinational organizations that are responsible for the provision of public goods and services on an international basis, have to be financed out of funds subscribed by member states, thereby adding to their public expenditure.

6. **Foreign aid:** Acceptance by the richer industrialized coun-

---

123   "Causes for Growth of public expenditure." Retrieved 20 February 2012.

tries of their responsibility to help the poor developing countries has channeled some of the increased public expenditure
of the donor country into foreign aid programmes.

7. **Inflation**: This is the general rise in price level of goods and
   services. It increases the cost of all activities of the public
   sector and thus a major factor in growth in money terms of
   public expenditure.

Chapter Four

SUBSIDIES

4.1. Introduction

A subsidy or government incentive is a form of financial aid or support extended to an economic sector (or institution, business, or individual) generally with the aim of promoting economic and social policy.[124] Although commonly extended from government, the term subsidy can relate to any type of support, for example from NGOs or as implicit subsidies. Subsidies come in various forms including: direct (cash grants, interest-free loans) and indirect (tax breaks, insurance, low-interest loans, accelerated depreciation, rent rebates).[125]

---

124   Myers, N.; Kent, J. (2001). Perverse subsidies: how tax dollars can undercut the environment and the economy. Washington, DC: Island Press.

125   Collins Dictionary of Economics."Retrieved 2013-09-05.Is That a Good State/Local Economic Development Deal? A Checklist (2014-06-03), Naked Capitalism

Furthermore, subsidies "can be broad or narrow, legal or illegal, ethical or unethical. The most common forms of subsidies are those to the producer or the consumer. Producer/production subsidies ensure producers are better off by supplying market price support, direct support, or payments to factors of production.[126] Consumer/consumption subsidies commonly reduce the price of goods and services to the consumer. For example, in the US at one time it was cheaper to buy gasoline than bottled water."[127]

Whether subsidies are positive or negative is typically a normative judgment. As a form of economic intervention, subsidies are inherently contrary to the market's demands. However, they can also be used as tools of political and corporate cronyism.

Although subsidies can be important, many are "perverse", in the sense of having adverse unintended consequences. To be "perverse", subsidies must exert effects that are demonstrably and significantly adverse both economically and environmentally.[128] A subsidy rarely, if ever, starts perverse, but over time a legitimate efficacious subsidy can become perverse or illegitimate if it is not withdrawn after meeting its goal or as political goals change. Perverse subsidies are now so widespread that as of 2007 they amounted $2 trillion per year in the six most subsidized sectors alone (agriculture, fossil fuels, road transportation, water, fisheries and forestry).[129]

---

126   Myers. Op. cit. Island Press.

127   Myers, N. (1998). "Lifting the veil on perverse subsidies". Nature. 392(6674): 327–328.

128   Myers. Op. cit. Island Press.

129   Myers, N. (1997). "Perverse Subsidies". In Costanza, R.; Norgaard, R.; Daly, H.; Goodland, R.; Cumberland, J. An introduction to ecological economics. Boca Raton, Fla.: St. Lucie Press. ISBN 1884015727.Retrieved 2013-08-03.

4.2. Definition of Subsidy

Subsidy, can be defined as benefits offered by the government to groups, individuals, or industry in various forms such as welfare payment, tax allowance, keep prices low, induce investment to reduce unemployment, and many more. It is also called 'subvention'. Objective of subsidy is often used to get rid of some burden and considered to be interest of the public. These subsidies should not be misused for any negative activities such as smuggling due to not wasting taxpayers' effort and hard work.

A subsidy is a financial payment made by the government to a business or economic sector, or producers. It is a benefit given to an individual, business or institution, usually by the government. It is usually in the form of a cash payment or a tax reduction. The subsidy is typically given to remove some type of burden, and it is often considered to be in the overall interest of the public, given to promote a social good or an economic policy.

A subsidy takes the form of a payment, provided directly or indirectly, which provides a concession to the receiving individual or business entity. A Subsidy is generally seen as a privileged type of financial aid, as it lessens an associated burden that was previously levied against the receiver, or promotes a particular action by providing financial support.

A subsidy typically supports particular sectors of a nation's economy. It can assist struggling industries by lowering the burdens placed on them, or encourage new developments by providing financial support for the endeavors. Often, these areas are not being effectively supported through the actions of the general economy, or may be undercut by activities in rival economies.

There are many forms of subsidies given out by the government. Two of the most common types of individual subsidies are welfare payments and unemployment benefits. The objective of these types of subsidies is to help people who are temporarily suffering economically. Other subsidies, such as student loans, are given to encourage people to further their education.

Subsidies to businesses are given to support an industry that is struggling against international competition that has lowered prices, such that the domestic business is not profitable without the subsidy.

In South Sudan the government subsidized supply of fuel. "The need for fuel price subsidy was explainable in the light of knowing how the whole market had been behaving following devaluation. Government adopted a 40% subsidy policy to protect the consumer against fuel price increases and to ensure availability of fuel on the market. The 40% subsidy meant that Government would provide SSP15 for every litre sold and the consumer would pay the balance of SSP22, which became a fixed pump price. However, the policy had assumed a movement of the subsidized price based on percentage; not based on a fixed price of SSP22 or US$0.14 as it turned out to be."[130]

The genesis of application of fuel price subsidy in South Sudan was the subsequent result of the devaluation of the national currency in December 2015.[131]

---

130   Sudan People's Liberation Movement-SPLM National Secretariat. Secretariat of Planning & Economic Affairs, SPLM National Economic Task-force (SPLM/NET). Brainstorming on NilePet Fuel Price Subsidy, October 23, 2017. P. 7.

131   Ibid. p. 13.

4.3 Purposes for Subsidies

Subsidies worldwide are given for the following reasons:

1. Direct payments to wheat, cotton, wool, and other agricultural producers are to ensure adequate production to meet domestic and foreign demand and to protect or supplement the income of farmers.
2. To prevent the decline of an industry and boost demand for industries during a recession such as the car scrap page scheme.
3. A subsidy may also be in the form of a project grant.
4. To encourage the sale of exports.
5. Subsidies on some foodstuffs to keep down the cost of living.
6. To encourage the expansion of production to achieve self-reliance.
7. To keep prices down and control inflation. In the last couple of years, several countries have been offering fuel subsidies to consumers and businesses in the wake of the steep increase in world crude oil prices.
8. To encourage consumption of merit goods and services which are said to generate positive externalities (increased social benefits). Examples might include subsidies for investment in environmental goods and services.
9. Reduce the cost of capital investment projects–which might help to stimulate economic growth by increasing long-run aggregate supply.
10. Subsidies to slow-down the process of long term decline in fishing or mining industry.

In international trade, subsidies to local producers are a form of trade protection because they make locally produced goods cheaper than imports.

A subsidy has a significant impact on the demand and supply of products and hence on their price. A subsidy that encourages production, for example, a subsidy to farmers, will increase supply and so shift the supply curve. A subsidy that reduces the price will increase demand. A change in demand and/or supply caused by a subsidy will result in a new economic equilibrium. Subsidies therefore affect the price, demand and supply or goods and services.

Like taxes, the recipient of subsidies should be distinguished from the beneficiary of the same subsidies. The recipient may not always be the beneficiary. Again like taxes, the distinction between the recipient and the beneficiary is determined by, among other factors, the elasticity of demand and supply.[132]

4.4. Types of Subsidies

There are different types of subsidies and they are:[133]

1. **Direct Subsidies**: Subsidies in form of or direct cash payments.
2. **Indirect Subsidies**: Non cash subsidies.
3. **Labour Subsidies**: Subsidies intended to help the recipient to pay labour costs or reduce the wage bill.
4. **Employment Subsidy**: An employment subsidy serves as an incentive to businesses to provide more job opportunities to reduce the level of unemployment in the country (income subsidies) or to encourage research and development.[134]
   With an employment subsidy, the government provides assistance with wages. Another form of employment subsidy

---

132   Saleemi. Op. cit. p. 265.

133   Ibid. pp. 265-266.

134   Collins Dictionary of Economics," Retrieved 2013-09-05.

is the social security benefits. Employment subsidies allow a person receiving the benefit to enjoy some minimum standard of living.

5. **Production Subsidies**: These are subsidies intended to encourage the growth of a particular industry. A production subsidy encourages suppliers to increase the output of a particular product by partially offsetting the production costs or losses.[135] The objective of production subsidies is to expand production of a particular product more so that the market would promote but without raising the final price to consumers. This type of subsidy is predominantly found in developed markets.[136] Other examples of production subsidies include the assistance in the creation of a new firm (Enterprise Investment Scheme), industry (industrial policy) and even the development of certain areas (regional policy). Production subsidies are critically discussed in the literature as they can cause many problems including the additional cost of storing the extra produced products, depressing world market prices, and incentivizing producers to over-produce, for example, a farmer overproducing in terms of his land's carrying capacity.

6. **Import Subsidies**: An import subsidy is support from the government for products that are imported. Though more rare, this subsidy further reduces the price to consumers for imported goods.

7. **Export Subsidies**: Payments and other incentives intended to make exports more competitive. An export subsidy is a support from the government for products that are exported,

---

135   Ibid.

136   Myers. Op. cit. Island Press.

as a means of assisting the country's balance of payments.[137]

8. **Consumption Subsidies**: Governments may provide subsidies by actually giving away a good or service, making available the use of government assets by private individuals or companies or charging a service at a lower price than its cost. A consumption subsidy is one that subsidizes the behavior of consumers. This type of subsidies are most common in developing countries where governments subsidize such things as food, water, electricity and education on the basis that no matter how impoverished, all should be allowed those most basic requirements. For example, some governments offer 'lifeline' rates for electricity, that is, the first increment of electricity each month is subsidized.[138]

9. **Tax Subsidy**: Government can create the same outcome through selective tax breaks as through cash payment.[139] For example, suppose a government sends monetary assistance that reimburses 15% of all health expenditures to a group that is paying 15% income tax. Exactly the same subsidy is achieved by giving a health tax deduction. Tax subsidies are also known as tax expenditures. Tax subsidies are one of the main explanations for why the American tax code is so complicated. Tax breaks are often considered to be a subsidy. Like other subsidies, they distort the economy; but tax breaks are also less transparent, and are difficult to undo.[140]

---

137   Collins Dictionary of Economics".Retrieved 2013-09-05.

138   Myers. Op. cit. Island Press.

139   Is That a Good State/Local Economic Development Deal? A Checklist (2014-06-03), Naked Capitalism

140   "Chapter 3: Subsidy types". Global Subsidies Initiative, IISD. Archived from the original on 2012-09-05.Retrieved 2015-05-03.

10. **Transport Subsidies**: Some governments subsidize transport, especially rail and bus transport which decrease congestion and pollution compared to cars. In the EU, rail subsidies are around EU73 billion and in China they reach $130 billion. Publicly owned airports can be an indirect subsidy if they lose money.[141]

In many countries, roads and highways are paid for through general revenue rather than tolls or other dedicated sources only paid by road users creating an indirect subsidy for road transportation. For instance, the fact that long distance buses in Germany do not pay tolls has been called a subsidy by critics pointing to track access charges for railways.

11. **Oil Subsidies**: An oil subsidy is one aimed at decreasing the overall price of oil. Oil subsidies have always played a major part in U.S. history. These began as early as World War I and have increased in the following decades. However, due to changes in the perceptions of the environment, in 2012 President Barack Obama ended the subsidies to the oil industry, which were, at the time, $4 billion.[142]

12. Housing Subsidies: Housing subsidies are designed to promote the construction industry and home ownership. As of 2018, housing subsidies total around $15 billion per year. Housing subsidies can come in two types; assistance with down payment and interest rate subsidies. The deduction of mortgage interest from the federal income tax accounts for the largest interest rate subsidy. Additionally, the

---

141　"China to Invest $128 Billion in Rail, Push for Global Share". Amadeo, Kimberly. "Government Subsidies (Farm, Oil, Export, etc.)". The Balance. Retrieved 03/16/2018.

142　Amadeo, Kimberly. "Government Subsidies (Farm, Oil, Export, etc.)". The Balance. Retrieved 03/16/2018.

federal government will help low income families with the down payment, coming to $10.9 million in 2008.[143] Removing energy subsidies is viewed as a necessary measure to combat greenhouse gas emissions as it helps decrease energy consumption.[144]

13. **Environmental Externalities**: As well as the conventional and formal subsidies as outlined above there are myriad implicit subsidies principally in the form of environmental externalities.[145] These subsidies include anything that is omitted but not accounted for and thus is an externality. These include things such as car drivers who pollute everyone's atmosphere without compensating everyone, farmers who use pesticides which can pollute everyone›s ecosystems again without compensating everyone, or Britain›s electricity production which results in additional acid rain in Scandinavia.[146] In these examples, the polluter is effectively gaining a net benefit but not compensating those affected. Although they are not subsidies in the form of direct economic support from the Government, they are no less economically, socially and environmentally harmful.

A 2015 report studied the implicit subsidies accruing to 20 fossil fuel companies and found that, while highly profit-

---

143   Ibid.

144   Indra Overland (2010) 'Subsidies for Fossil Fuels and Climate Change: A Comparative Perspective', International Journal of Environmental Studies, Vol. 67, No. 3, pp. 203-217. https://www.researchgate.net/publication/240515305

145   Myers, N. (1998). "Lifting the veil on perverse subsidies". Nature. 392(6674): 327–328. doi:10.1038/32761.

146   Myers, N. (1998). "Lifting the veil on perverse subsidies". Nature. 392(6674): 327–328. doi:10.1038/32761. Myers, N. (2008). "Perverse Priorities" (PDF). IUCN Opinion Piece: 6–7.

able, the hidden economic cost to society was also large.[147] The report spans the period 2008–2012 and notes that: "for all companies and all years, the economic cost to society of their CO_2 emissions was greater than their after-tax profit, with the single exception of Exxon Mobil in 2008.[148]

Pure coal companies fare even worse: "the economic cost to society exceeds total revenue (employment, taxes, supply purchases, and indirect employment) in all years, with this cost varying between nearly $2 and nearly $9 per $1 of revenue.[149]

14. **Ad valorem Subsidies**: Ad valorem taxes are given as percentage of price or a percentage value of a product. When the price or value of the item changes, the amount received as subsidy changes.

15. **Specific Subsidies**: Specific subsidies are given as a fixed amount per unit of a product irrespective of its value. For example, if 10 piastres subsidy is given to bakers of bread, each loaf is subsidized at 10 piastres irrespective of the cost and price of the bread.

---

147   Hope, Chris; Gilding, Paul; Alvarez, Jimena (2015). Quantifying the implicit climate subsidy received by leading fossil fuel companies — Working Paper No. 02/2015 (PDF). Cambridge, UK: Cambridge Judge Business School, University of Cambridge. Retrieved 2016-06-27."Measuring fossil fuel 'hidden' costs". University of Cambridge Judge Business School. 23 July 2015. Retrieved 2016-06-27.

148   Myers, N.; Kent, J. (2001). Op. cit.

149   Hope, Chris; Gilding, Paul; Alvarez, Jimena (2015). Quantifying the implicit climate subsidy received by leading fossil fuel companies — Working Paper No. 02/2015 (PDF). Cambridge, UK: Cambridge Judge Business School, University of Cambridge. Retrieved 2016-06-27.Myers, N.; Kent, J. (2001). Perverse subsidies: how tax dollars can undercut the environment and the economy. Washington, DC: Island Press. ISBN 1-55963-835-4. Myers, N. (1998). "Lifting the veil on perverse subsidies". Nature. 392(6674): 327–328. doi:10.1038/32761.

16. Agricultural Subsidies: Support for agriculture dates back to the 19th century. It was developed extensively in the EU and USA across the two World Wars and the Great Depression to protect domestic food production, but remains important across the world today.[150] In 2005, US farmers received $14 billion and EU farmers $47 billion in agricultural subsidies.[151] Today, agricultural subsidies are defended on the grounds of helping farmers to maintain their livelihoods. The majority of payments is based on outputs and inputs and thus favours the larger producing agribusinesses over the small-scale farmers.[152] In the USA nearly 30% of payments go to the top 2% of farmers.[153] By subsidizing inputs and outputs through such schemes as 'yield based subsidization', farmers are encouraged to: over-produce using intensive methods including using more fertilizers and pesticides; grow high-yielding mono-

---

150   Robin, S.; Wolcott, R.; Quintela, C.E. (2003). Perverse Subsidies and the Implications for Biodiversity: A review of recent findings and the status of policy reforms(PDF). Durban, South Africa: Vth World Parks Congress: Sustainable Finance Stream. Archived from the original (PDF) on 2013-12-03.Myers, N. (1996). "Perverse Subsidies" (PDF). Sixth Ordinary Meeting of the Conference of the Parties to the Convention on Biological Diversity: 268–278.

151   Kolb, R.W. (2008). "Subsidies". Encyclopedia of business ethics and society. Thousand Oaks: Sage Publications. ISBN 9781412916523.

152   Myers. Op. cit. Island Press. ISBN 1-55963-835-4. Steenblik, R. (1998). "Previous Multilateral Efforts to Discipline Subsidies to Natural Resource Based Industries" (PDF). Workshop on the Impact of Government Financial Transfers on Fisheries Management, Resource Sustainability, and International Trade. Retrieved 2013-08-05.

153   Robin, S.; Wolcott, R.; Quintela, C.E. (2003). Perverse Subsidies and the Implications for Biodiversity: A review of recent findings and the status of policy reforms(PDF). Durban, South Africa: Vth World Parks Congress: Sustainable Finance Stream. Archived from the original (PDF) on 2013-12-03.How Farm Subsidies Harm Taxpayers, Consumers, and Farmers, Too. Who Benefits from Farm Subsidies?

cultures; reduce crop rotation; shorten fallow periods; and promote exploitative land use change from forests, rainforests and wetlands to agricultural land.[154] These all lead to severe environmental degradation including adverse effects on: soil quality and productivity including erosion, nutrient supply and salinity which in turn affects carbon storage and cycling, water retention and drought resistance; water quality including pollution, nutrient deposition and eutrophication of waterways, and lowering of water tables; diversity of flora and fauna including indigenous species both directly and indirectly through the destruction of habitats, resulting in a genetic wipe-out.[155]

Cotton growers in the US reportedly receive half their income from the government under the Farm Bill of 2002. The subsidy payments stimulated overproduction and resulted in a record cotton harvest in 2002, much of which had to be sold at much reduced prices in the global market.[156]For foreign producers, the depressed cotton price lowered their prices far below the break-even price. In fact, African farmers received 35 to 40 cents per pound for cotton, while US cotton growers, backed by government agricultural payments, and received 75 cents per pound. Developing countries and trade

---

154   Robin, S.; Wolcott, R.; Quintela, C.E. Op. cit.. Archived from the original (PDF) on 2013-12-03.

155   Myers. Ibid. Island Press. Robin, S.; Wolcott, R.; Quintela, C.E. Ibid. The OECD Workshop on Environmentally Harmful Subsidies, Paris, 7–8 November 2002.OECD (2003). "Perverse incentives in biodiversity loss" (PDF). Working Party on Global and Structural Policies Working Group on Economic Aspects of Biodiversity. Retrieved 2013-08-05.

156   Kolb, R.W. (2008). "Subsidies". Encyclopedia of business ethics and society. Thousand Oaks: Sage Publications. ISBN 9781412916523.

organizations argue that poorer countries should be able to export their principal commodities to survive, but protectionist laws and payments in the United States and Europe prevent these countries from engaging in international trade opportunities.

17. **Fisheries Subsidies**: Today, much of the world's major fisheries is overexploited, and is estimated at approximately 75%. Fishing subsidies include "direct assistant to fishers; loan support programs; tax preferences and insurance support; capital and infrastructure programs; marketing and price support programs; and fisheries management, research, and conservation programs."[157]

They promote the expansion of fishing fleets, the supply of larger and longer nets, larger yields and indiscriminate catch, as well as mitigating risks which encourages further investment into large-scale operations to the disfavour of the already struggling small-scale industry.[158] Collectively, these result in the continued overcapitalization and overfishing of marine fisheries.

There are four categories of fisheries subsidies. First, are direct financial transfers. Second, are indirect financial transfers and services. Third, certain forms of intervention and fourth, not intervening. The first category regards direct payments from the government received by the fisheries industry. These typically affect profits of the industry in the short term and can be negative or positive. Category two pertains to

---

157   Robin, S.; Wolcott, R.; Quintela, C.E. Op. cit. p. 4.

158   Robin, S.; Wolcott, R.; Quintela, C.E. Op. cit. Porter, G. (1998). "Natural Resource Subsidies, Trade and Environment: The Cases of Forest and Fisheries" (PDF). Center for Environmental Law. Retrieved 2013-08-05.

government intervention, not involving those under the first category. These subsidies also affect the profits in the short term but typically are not negative. Category three, regards intervention that results in a negative short-term economic impact, but economic benefits in the long term. These benefits are usually more general societal benefits such as the environment. The final category pertains to inaction by the government, allowing producers to impose certain production costs on others. These subsidies tend to lead to positive benefits in the short term but negative in the long term.[159]

18. **Other Subsidies**: The US National Football League's (NFL) profits have topped records at $11 billion, the highest of all sports. The NFL had tax-exempt status until voluntarily relinquishing it in 2015, and new stadiums have been built with public subsidies.[160]

The Commitment to Development Index (CDI), published by the Center for Global Development, measures the effect that subsidies and trade barriers actually have on the undeveloped world. It uses trade, along with six other components such as aid or investment, to rank and evaluate developed countries on policies that affect the undeveloped world. It finds that the richest countries spend $106 billion per year subsidizing their own

---

159   "Report of the Expert Consultation on Identifying, Assessing and Reporting on Subsidies in the Fishing Industry - Rome, 3-6 December 2002". Food and Agriculture Organization of the United Nations. Food and Agriculture Organization. Retrieved 03/16/2018.

160   https://www.wsj.com/articles/nfl-to-end-tax-exempt-status-1430241845?mod=e2twCohen, R. (2008). "Playing by the NFL's Tax Exempt Rulesh". Non Profit Quarterly. Retrieved 2013-04-15.

farmers, almost exactly as much as they spend on foreign aid.[161]

4.5. Categories of Subsidies

These various subsidies can be divided into broad and narrow:

1. Broad subsidies include both monetary and non-monetary subsidies and are often difficult to identify.[162] A broad subsidy is less attributable and less transparent. Environmental externalities are the most common type of broad subsidy.

2. Narrow subsidies are those monetary transfers that are easily identifiable and have a clear intent. They are commonly characterized by a monetary transfer between governments and institutions or businesses and individuals. A classic example is a government payment to a farmer.[163]

4.6. Advantages and Disadvantages of Subsidies

Subsidies have advantages and disadvantages and they are:

4.6.1. Advantages of Subsidies

1. Economists who promote a mixed economy often argue that subsidies are justifiable to provide the "socially optimal" level of goods and services. In contemporary neoclassical economic models, there are circumstances where the actual supply of a good or service falls below the theoretical equilibrium level, an unwanted shortage, which creates what economists call a "market failure." One form of correcting this imbalance is to

---

161   Fowler, P.; Fokker, R. (2004). A Sweeter Future? The potential for EU sugar reform to contribute to poverty reduction in Southern Africa. Oxford: Oxfam International. ISBN 9781848141940.

162   Myers, N. (2008). "Perverse Priorities" (PDF). IUCN Opinion Piece: 6–7.

163   Myers. Op. cit. pp. 6–7.

subsidize the good or service being under supplied. The subsidy lowers the cost for the producers to bring the good or service to market. If the right level of subsidization is provided, all other things being equal, the market failure should be corrected. In other words, according to general equilibrium theory, subsidies are necessary when a market failure causes too little production in a specific area: they would theoretically push production back up to optimal levels.

2. There are many goods or services that allegedly provide what economists call "positive externalities." A positive externality is achieved whenever a transaction between two parties provides an indirect benefit to a third party. Many subsidies are implemented to promote positive externalities that might not otherwise be provided at the socially optimal threshold.

3. Some theories of development argue that the governments of less developed countries should subsidize domestic industries in their infancy to protect them from international competition. This is a popular technique seen in China and various South American nations currently.

    a. Control of Inflation: In the last couple of years several countries have been offering fuel subsidies to consumers and businesses in the wake of the steep increase in world crude oil prices.

    b. Merit goods and services generate positive externalities, increased benefits. Examples include subsidies for investment in environmental goods and services.

    c. Reduce the cost of capital investment projects which might help to stimulate economic growth by increasing long run aggregate supply. Subsidies to slow down the process of long term decline in an industry e.g. fishing and mining. Subsidies to boost demand for industries during a recession e.g. the car scrap page scheme.

4.6.2. Disadvantages of Subsidies

1. Free market economists are wary of subsidies for a variety of reasons. Some argue that subsidies unnecessarily distort markets, preventing efficient outcomes and diverting resources from more productive uses to less productive ones. Similar concerns come from those who suggest economic calculation is too inexact and microeconomic models are too unrealistic to ever correctly calculate the impact of market failure. Others suggest that government spending on subsidies is never as effective as government projections claim they will be. The costs and unintended consequences of applying subsidies are rarely worth it, they claim.

2. Another problem, antagonists say: the act of subsidizing helps corrupt the political process. According to political theories of regulatory capture and rent seeking subsidies exist as part of an unholy alliance between big business and the state. Companies often turn to government to shield themselves from competition. In turn, businesses donate to politicians or promise them benefits after their political careers.

3. Even if a subsidy is created with good intentions, without any conspiracy or self-seeking, it raises the profits of those receiving beneficial treatment, and so creates an incentive to lobby for its continuance, even after the need or its usefulness runs out. This potentially allows political and business interests to create a mutual benefit at the expense of taxpayers and/or competitive firms or industries.

4. Could be funded through an increase in taxes

5. Increase in borrowing-opportunity cost.
6. Take money from other parts of Government spending.
7. Distorts the free market mechanism.
8. Could lead to inefficient producers.
9. Costs of the subsidy could exceed the benefits.

4.7. The Incidence of a Subsidy

As already mentioned, there is a difference between the recipient and the beneficiary of a subsidy.

Direct subsidies consist of direct cash payments by government to private producers and consumers. A subsidy to a producer reduces the cost of production of such a product and as such shifts the supply curve downwards. This means that more output is supplied. As a result, prices fall and demand increases.

The sharing of the benefits and costs of a subsidy depends on the elasticity of demand and elasticity of supply for the product being subsidized.[164]

4.8. Arguments against Subsidies

The decision for provision of a subsidy by the government need to be judged carefully on the grounds of efficiency and fairness. The money that's going to be spent on subsidy payments may be better to be spent elsewhere because government subsidies carry an opportunity cost. Whereas, in the long run there might be better ways of providing financial support to producers and workers in specific industries. Some free market economists argue that subsidies distort the functioning of the free market mechanism and can lead to government failure where intervention leads to a worse distribution of resources. Hence, the following are points

---

164   Mutamba. Op. cit. pp. 266-267.

against the subsidies:

1. Distortion of the Market: Subsidies distort market prices, for example, export subsidies distort the trade in goods and services and can curtail the ability of ELDCs to compete in the markets of rich nations.
2. Arbitrary Assistance: Decisions about who receives a subsidy can be arbitrary, based on political aims.
3. Financial Cost: Subsidies can become expensive in the long run–note the opportunity cost.
4. Who Pays and Who Benefits? The final cost of a subsidy falls on consumers (or taxpayers) who themselves may have derived no benefit from the subsidy.
5. Encouraging Inefficiency: Subsidy can artificially protect inefficient firms who need to restructure, i.e., it delays much needed reforms.
6. Risk Fraud: Ever present risk of fraud when allocating subsidy payments (the system of cap farm subsidies have been heavily criticized for the level of fraud involved).
7. There are Alternatives: It may be possible to achieve the objectives of subsidies by alternative means which have less distorting effects.
8. Subsidies used in isolation are less effective than if part of strategic integrated solution to a particular economic/social problem.

Chapter Five

The National Budget

5.1. Concept of a National Budget

The national budget is a financial statement that gives an estimate of the planned revenue and planned expenditure of a country for a given year. The national budget provides an analysis of how the government plans to raise revenue, how much is expected from each source and how the money will be spent in a given financial year. The national budget also provides information about:[165]

1. How revenue is going to be realized and ways of spending it.
2. The socio-economic policy to be implemented.
3. Projections about the rate of economic growth.

---

165   Mutamba. Op. cit. p. 267.

4. Priority areas of major government expenditure.
5. Estimated volume of foreign exchange earnings from exports.
6. Give position and policy about the public debt.
7. Spell the fiscal, monetary and direct policies to be implemented.
8. The volume of output of the major sectors.
9. The national budget is made and presented to parliament by the Minister of Finance or any other official depending on the country before the new financial year begins. Parliament then debates and approves the budget before it can be implemented.

5.2. Objectives of a Budget

The budget is a major tool by which the government regulates the economy by allocating expenditure and revenue in a way that will ensure the achievement of desired macroeconomic objectives. The budget is used to achieve any of the following objectives:[166]

1. The budget is used to achieve price stability: A surplus budget controls inflation while a deficit budget solves deflation. A proper balance puts the economy at the desired price levels.
2. To redistributes incomes among individuals, sectors, and regions of the economy. For example, income inequality among individuals is solved through the budgeting process by raising revenue in form of taxation from high income groups and then spending the raised revenue on the low income groups.
3. Protects domestic industries from foreign competition: This

---

166   Ibid. pp. 269-270.

is normally done by subsidizing local industries and taxing imports.

4. Promotes economic growth by allocating more money to infrastructure, export promotion, education and industrial sector.

5. A budget is used as a tool to correct balance of payments disequilibrium. High taxes on imports, subsidies to exporters and export promotion initiatives are used to achieve this.

6. Raises sufficient revenue from internal and external sources to fund government expenditure.

7. Leads to a reduction in national poverty levels by ensuring proper allocation of resources.

8. Ensures the efficient and sustainable use of national resources towards sectors that assist the poor.

9. Creates employment opportunities: This is done by reducing corporate taxes on labour intensive firms, subsidizing wage bills and setting up investments that absorb excess labour.

10. The national budget is a tool for national accountability. The leaders explain how funds are to be used and how national resources are being used and managed.

11. The national budget attracts foreign investors because they are able to know how the economy is performing, what incentives are available, what sectors are being promoted, and the regulatory policies in place.

12. Donors support poor countries based on their budgetary needs. A good budget therefore enables the country to obtain foreign financial assistance. Donor assistance is at times referred to as a budget support.

It should be noted that the objectives of a national budget vary depending on the goals of the government at a particular time.

5.3. Types of Budgets

There are two types of budgets namely, the balanced and the unbalanced budget.[167]

1. **The Balanced Budget**: It is a budget in which expected revenue from taxation is equal to expected expenditure. There is no expected surplus or deficit.

2. **The Unbalanced Budget**: The government may deliberately draw an unbalanced budget where expected revenue from taxation is not equal to expected expenditure. There are two forms of unbalanced budget and they are:

a. **Surplus Budget**: A surplus budget exists when the expected revenue from taxes is greater than expected expenditure. A budget surplus exists when the total government revenue from taxation is greater than what the government plans to spend in a financial year. While the government may plan a surplus budget as a means of accumulating reserve for other years, it may be used to reduce money supply and aggregate demand if the country is faced with inflation. In addition, a surplus budget may be used to reduce the country's dependence on other countries in terms of budget support.

b. **Deficit Budget**: A deficit budget exists when the expected government revenue from taxation is less than expected government expenditure. A deficit budget which is deliberately made to increase aggregate demand, expand economic activity and employment is called a structural deficit. A deficit due to changes in economic activity like reduced income, collapse of revenue generating sectors is called a cyclical deficit.

---

167   Ibid. pp. 267-269.

5.4. Reasons for Deficit Financing

Government budget does not always balance. The government may deliberately operate a deficit budget or a surplus budget. Deficit financing may be undertaken for the following reasons:

1. Encourage private investment reducing taxes while increasing expenditure on subsidies and provision of services and infrastructure.
2. Promote employment by encouraging production methods that use labour intensive methods. This involves reducing taxes and financing training.
3. Deficit financing stimulates the economy out of a depression and causes mild inflation, which in turn encourages investment and entrepreneurship.
4. Avoid taxes that may be politically unacceptable. This is normally done during election times. Reducing taxes also stimulates aggregate demand to increase which is essential for the economy to grow.
5. The low taxable capacity in the developing countries makes it hard for government to raise sufficient revenue from taxation in order to get all the funds it requires to finance its expenditure therefore, the government must resort to non-tax sources.
6. Raising revenue from internal and external borrowing rather than raising taxes is much cheaper and more convenient.

5.5. Problems of Deficit Financing

Deficit financing may however be faced by the following problems:

1. It may cause inflation.
2. Foreign sources of funding are not guaranteed.

3. It expands the national debts.
4. Accumulated reserves may be depleted if the deficit financing is done year after year.

5.6. Alternative Sources for Financing Deficit Budget

For the government to operate a deficit budget, it must have alternative sources of revenue rather than taxes. The deficit may be financed by:

1. Borrowing from internal and external lenders. These may be banks, individuals, governments, private firms and international financial institutions.
2. Use of accumulated reserves. A country that has had a surplus budget in previous years may use the funds accumulated to finance a deficit in the current year.
3. Accumulating domestic and foreign arrears may finance a deficit budget. The government obtains goods and services on credit and promises to pay in other years and not the current budget year.
4. Sell gold reserves of the country to finance the deficit.

5.7. Problems of Budgeting

Making a national budget is not a simple process. This is because all sectors of the economy, all regions and all departments have to be involved. Different regions and sectors have unique problems and needs all of which demand for allocation of funds during the budgeting process. The problems and complexity of the budgeting process explain why the budget, even when it has been drawn, presented, debated and passed, may have to be re-adjusted to cater for unforeseen occurrences, cater for under estimations and omissions. The problems facing the budgeting process especially in developing countries are as follows:[168]

1. **Inadequate Skilled Personnel**: There is inadequate skilled manpower to collect data and draw the national budget in proper consideration of all the needs of all the sectors and regions of the country.

2. **Balancing the Budget**: Most developing countries face the problem of balancing limited resources of revenue and many areas that require expenditure. Because of poverty and low incomes, revenue from taxation is low yet at the same time, the poor people need services in form of medical care and education.

3. **Development Oriented** deficit budgets are inflationary: Deficit budgets lead to lower taxes and this leads to more money getting into public hands. This may cause an increase in aggregate demand and hence inflation. Inflation has the effect of changing the purchasing power of money therefore the budgeted revenue may in the end fail to purchase and pay for goods and services budgeted for, this causes a short fall not because money collected is not enough but because of price changes.

4. **Unpredictable Sources of Revenue**: Unforeseen occurrences often interfere with revenue collections. For example, political instability reduces income tax which reduces tax revenue. When the planned revenue is not realized, then implementing the budget becomes very difficult.

5. **Corruption**: During the budgeting process, which determines the way national resources are to be allocated, political and tribal considerations often outweigh economic and na-

---

168   Ibid. pp. 270–272.

tional considerations. Corruption results in allocations that favour certain groups and regions leaving out those that are in most need. For example, funds may be allocated to build roads in a certain region because the leaders of government come from that region and not because that region is the most economically productive. This reduces the importance of budgeting as a tool for balanced development.

6. **Inconsistency in Policy due to Change in Government**: When a government changes, a new regime comes in with its own programmes. Revenue sources are abandoned. Long term projects that span many years are therefore bound not to be effected.

7. **Political Instability**: Political instability creates emergency expenditure that may not have been budgeted for. In addition, political instability leads to diversion of large amounts of funds into military expenditure at the expense of development.

8. **Change in Foreign Policy**: A change in a country's foreign policy and foreign relations affects the inflow of budget support from donors and development partners. This reduces the inflow of foreign funds in form of grants, loans, and assistance to finance the budget.

9. **Change in Exchange Rates**: When the country's currency depreciates, it grossly affects government plans since the money collected may not adequately finance the budgeted expenditure.

10. **Donor Pressure and Dependency**: Most developing countries have full economic independence and take advice from donors in terms of how to allocate expenditure. The country may at times have to spend not where it feels there

is need but where the donors wish. For example, most countries are prohibited from increasing expenditure on defense even when faced with war. The interests and views of the donors therefore tend to take precedence over the interests of the country's leaders.

11. **Natural Hazards and Emergencies**: When an emergency occurs, funds must be made available to finance it. This often means diverting resources from one sector to another. For example, in case of an outbreak of an epidemic, funds are diverted from education, agriculture, and road construction to handling the epidemic. This distorts the functioning of the entire system.

Chapter Six

❖

The National Budget Of South Sudan

6.1. Background

The fiscal year of the Republic of South Sudan begins on 1ˢᵗ July and ends on 30ᵗʰ June. There is a Budget Cycle for South Sudan. The Budget Cycle has four phases: Planning, Budgeting, Budget Execution and Monitoring, Reporting and Audit.[169] The figure below shows the Budget Cycle to be followed during the period of National Strategic Goals for the financial years 2018/19 to 2020/2021.[170]

---

169   Republic of South Sudan, National Development Strategy. Consolidate Peace and Stabilize the Economy, July 2018-June 2021. P.55.

170   Ibid. P. 55.

Figure 6.1: Budget Process and Budget Cycle

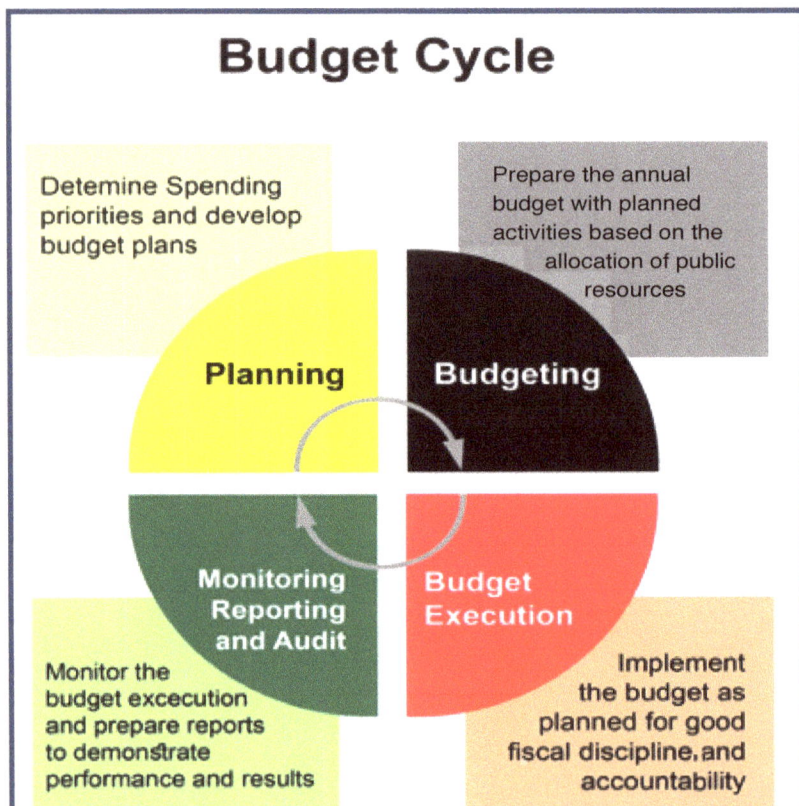

Budget Cycle

Detemine Spending priorities and develop budget plans

Prepare the annual budget with planned activities based on the allocation of public resources

Planning

Budgeting

Monitoring Reporting and Audit

Budget Execution

Monitor the budget excecution and prepare reports to demonstrate performance and results

Implement the budget as planned for good fiscal discipline, and accountability

Source: Republic of South Sudan. National Development Strategy: Consolidate Peace and Stabilize the Economy (July 2018-June 2021). P. 55.

6.2. Functions of the Government of South Sudan

A strong capable State is required to deliver Governments' priorities. Government of Southern Sudan (GoSS} in its inception in 2005 identified six priority core State functions which need immediate, continuous and intensive focus to ensure significant progress is made in 2011. These core functions are being carried on by the Government of South Sudan and they are:[171]

1. **Executive Leadership**: Effective leadership at the highest level of government is needed so that a clear vision can be defined, translated into plans, and communicated.

2. **Security Sector**: Central to managing stability in Southern Sudan will be the process of transforming the SPLA into a professional army.

3. **Rule of Law and Law Enforcement**: Justice and the rule of law are essential prerequisites for enabling economic development and delivery of services.

4. **Fiduciary Management**: Effective management of financial resources is a necessary condition for effective delivery of services and ensuring the trust of the population.

5. **Public Administration**: Improved civil service/human resource management is crucial for any effective and responsive government.

6. **Management of Natural Resources**: Effective oversight and management arrangements for key resources such as oil are essential.

6.3. Government of Southern Sudan Development Priorities

The six top expenditure priorities of the Government of Southern Sudan for the period 2008-2011 are:[172]

1. Security
2. Roads

---

171   Republic of South Sudan. The Approved National Budget Plan and the Approved Budget 2013/14. Ministry of Finance, Commerce, Investment and Economic Planning. P. 8.

172   Ibid. P.8.

Table: 6.1. Shows the Approved Budget for Fiscal Year 2011

	2005 outturn SDG equiv	2006 outturn SDG equiv	2007 outturn SDG equiv	2008 outturn	2009 outturn	2010 outturn (provisional)	2011 Approved Budget
Revenue	**1,869,722,079**	**2,736,099,414**	**2,977,805,178**	**6,789,576,441**	**4,239,803,630**	**5,756,840,579**	**5,767,110,495**
Oil Revenue	1,869,075,124	2,732,921,443	2,964,530,210	6,670,924,370	4,121,464,187	5,630,253,974	5,656,364,677
Non-Oil Revenue	464,954	3,178,001	13,274,969	118,652,071	118,339,443	126,586,605	110,745,818
Expenditure	**452,286,139**	**3,581,548,512**	**2,936,495,552**	**5,712,662,066**	**4,234,653,769**	**5,576,100,547**	**5,767,110,495**
Salaries	35,456,486	1,185,733,716	1,479,751,066	1,873,440,153	1,977,349,566	2,205,676,172	2,433,391,475
Operating	402,176,606	1,438,197,773	1,058,416,888	2,227,295,738	1,255,266,702	2,279,567,567	2,075,522,856
Capital	14,653,047	957,617,023	398,327,598	1,611,926,175	1,002,037,501	1,090,856,808	1,258,196,164
Balance	**1,417,435,939**	**-845,449,099**	**41,309,626**	**1,076,914,375**	**5,149,861**	**180,740,032**	**0**
GONU Direct Expenditures	191,062,926	81,110,731	88,623,360	23,424	3,087	166,721,262	-
Residual/ Exchange Loss	15,541,487	5,410,298	-	65,321,052	-	-	0
Reserves/ Deficit	1,210,831,526	-931,970,128	-47,313,734	987,881,899	5,146,774	14,018,770	
Memo Items							
Transfers to States	231,121,152	525,546,238	631,610,393	637,602,757	1,089,895,729	1,219,072,203	1,526,950,618
Transfers to Development Projects	-	139,188,037	93,432,562	136,249,863	-	4,600,000	4,300,000

Source: Government of Southern Sudan Approved Budget 2011. Ministry of Finance and Planning: Approved by Southern Sudan Legislative Assembly on 14th March 2011. [GoSS Revenues and Expenditures: 2005-2011]. P.2.

3. Primary Health care
4. Basic Education
5. Water; and
6. Production.

6.4. The Budgets of the Republic of South Sudan from 2011–2017

6.4.1 The Budget of the Fiscal Year 2011

Until the time South Sudan became independent on July 9, 2011, the Ministry of Finance continued to allocate resources in its 2011 Budget for both six top expenditure priorities and the priority core State functions. This was done in order to strengthen GoSS' capability to address key service delivery and development priorities.

GoSS' development priorities in 2011 budget were revised through GoSS Development Plan process, which was in turn to guide Post Referendum budgetary allocations. The Plan was structured around the four Pillars of Governance: Economic Growth, Human and Social Development, and Security and Conflict Resolution. Table 6.1. shows the approved budget of 2011.

6.4.2. The Budget of the Fiscal Year 2012/13

The budget of 2012/13 was in trouble due to the shutdown of the oil. As a result of the shutdown of oil, austerity policies were introduced. Significant cuts in expenditures across all elements of the budget were made. In light of the still precarious financial situation, and to prevent a deterioration of economic conditions, the austerity measures adopted for fiscal year 2012/13 were to be continued until at least the end of December 2013. As there was no petroleum sale to contribute to government revenues, considerable effort was to be made to improve collection of non-oil revenue. "The effort yielded good results with steady monthly growth in revenue from SSP35 million in February 2012 to approximately SSP70 million per month"[173] for other months of the year 2012.

Moreover, the Ministry of Finance, Commerce, Industry, and Economic Planning took on "a considerable debt to bridge the fiscal gap created by the fall in oil revenues. This was the first borrowing of any kind that the government has under taken and has been crucial for maintaining the basic functions of government...Debt has accumulated over the course of Fiscal Year 2012/13, estimated to total almost SSP4 billion by the end of the year.[174] The government has put "in place procedures to ensure effective debt management."[175]

During the interim period spending was focused on security and peace building, and the 2012/13 austerity period reinforced this. The emphasis on security and peace building had also meant that the budget was dominated by salaries, with 60% of budget allocations to government employees in 2012/13. Of this, 45% of the national budget was taken up by the salaries of national level employees and 15% transfers to state level salaries. Organized forces and defense comprised 80% of salary spending on national employees, and 70% of salary spending on state employees. Reducing public sector employment over the medium term was key to enable South Sudan to allocate more of its funds to

---

173   Republic of South Sudan, Ministry of Finance and Economic Planning. Approved Budget, Financial Year 2014/15 (August 2014). P. 14.

174   Ibid. p. 15.

175   Ibid. p. 16.

service delivery and investment.[176]

6.4.3. The Budget of the Fiscal Year 2013/14

The government was to continue to pursue activities to enhance non-oil revenue collection by building capacity and setting up appropriate collection and monitoring systems. As a result, a plan was initiated "to increase non-oil tax and customs revenue by more than 100 per cent in fiscal year 2013/14."[177]

In the year 2013/14 budget, the Ministry of Finance and Economic Planning made the National Budget Plan (NBP) which was the country's budget strategy required by the Public Financial Management and Accountability Act of 2011. The Plan contained proposals for implementing the Government's Policies as laid out in the South Sudan Development Plan (SSDP) through the annual budget.[178]

The NBP covered three key areas:[179]
1. The Government's macroeconomic policies, including the available revenues and fiscal strategy for the forthcoming financial year;
2. The overall expenditure priorities for 2013/14; and
3. Explanation of significant changes compared with the 2012/13 budget.

The total of all revenues projected to be available to the Government of South Sudan for fiscal year 2013/14 was SSP17.5 billion. This was the sum of SSP10.41 billion gross oil revenues,

---

176   Ibid. p. 18.

177   Ibid. p. 14.

178   Republic of South Sudan. The Approved National Budget Plan and the Approved Budget 2013/14. Ministry of Finance, Commerce, Investment and Economic Planning. P. 8.

179   Ibid. p. 8.

SSP1.96 billion from non-oil revenue, SSP0.35 billion from do-nor grants and SSP4.92 billion from loan financing.[180]

There was a short fall in non-oil revenue, donor grants and this forced spending reduction and this made obligations of some months during the year to be deferred until the beginning of the following fiscal year which ultimately had impact on the 2014/15 budget execution. Below is table 6.2 which shows sum-mary budget execution for the year 2013/14.

Table 6.2: Shows the Summary of 2013/14 Budget Execution:

	2013/14 Sup. Budget	2013/14 Provisional Outturns	Variance
Oil Revenue			
Oil Production Revenue	10,411	9,965	(446)
Oil Lease Revenue	–	74	–
Gross Oil Revenue	**10,411**	**10,039**	**(446)**
Oil Payment to Sudan	3,087	2,589	(498)
2%-3% for oil producing States/ communities	352	213	(139)
Net Oil Revenue	**6,972**	**7,237**	**191**
Non-Oil Revenue Total	**1,972**	**951**	**(1,016)**
Grants from Donors	**350**	**-**	**(350)**
Financing			
New Borrowing	4,914	5,647	733
Loan Repayments (Principal)	3,800	4,906	1,106

---

180   Ibid. p. 16.

Net Financing	1,114	741	(373)
Total Resources Available	10,403	8,929	(1,331)
Total Spending	10.403	8,929	(1,474)
Surplus/Deficit	-	(143)	(143)

Source: Republic of South Sudan,
Ministry of Finance and Economic Planning. Approved Budget,
Financial Year 2014/15 (August 2014). P. 6.

From table 6.2, net oil revenue was SSP265 million more than budgeted even though production was lower than projected.

Non-oil revenue increased slightly from that of 2012/2013 to SSP951 million but was less than half of the budgeted amount, with a total shortfall of SSP1,016 million. A portion of the shortfall can be attributed to the conflict which began in 2013 but lack of resources for the operations of the Taxation Directorate and other administrative issues also contributed to the shortfall. Donor grants to the budget did not materialize after the conflict began and net financing from loans was SSP373 million less than the projected.[181]

The resources available during the second half of the 2013/14 budget year were to be used to reverse some of the austerity measures imposed following the loss of oil revenue, and to address South Sudan Development Plan priorities. The priorities were:[182]

1. **Reversal of certain austerity cuts**: The austerity budget 2012/13 included a 50% reduction in housing allowances

---

181   Republic of South Sudan, Ministry of Finance and Economic Planning. Approved Budget, Financial Year 2014/15 (August 2014). P. 6.

182   Ibid. p. 18.

for all government employees. A priority was to undo this reduction beginning in January 2014. In addition there was a reverse of the 25% reduction in block transfers to enable states to deliver services to the citizens. These restorations were to cost SSP541 million for six months.[183]

2. **South Sudan Development Plan Priorities**: The second priority was to increase the portion of the budget devoted to South Sudan Development Plan priorities by devoting SSP1.1 billion to improvement of service delivery for the people of South Sudan in education, health and water especially in rural areas; the rapid development of infrastructure to support economic development and the creation of jobs in the agriculture and non-oil sectors of the economy.

3. **Other Priorities**: Additional priorities include the payment of interest obligations on loans, absorption of opposition armed groups into the defense forces, financing for embassies and a number of other priorities.[184]

The 2013/14 budget proposed SSP9.7 billion. The largest increase in both South Sudanese Pounds and percentage was for the infrastructure sector which was more than triple in the budget from SSP160 million in 2012/13 to SSP566 million in 2013/14, an increase of SSP406 million, representing the decision to build new roads and other essential projects. The next largest percentage increase was for the health sector, which doubled the budget from SSP192 million to SSP424 million. Block transfers increased by 49% from SSP650 million to SSP971 million as the austerity measure reduction was rescinded and new

---

183   Ibid. pp. 18–19.

184   Ibid. p. 19.

programmes instituted to improve services to communities. The share of the budget dedicated to security and Rule of Law decreased from 58% to 46%, freeing up funds for infrastructure and other development priorities.[185]

Table 6.3: Shows the Summary of Expenditure by Chapter for the Fiscal Years 2012/13-2013/14

Chapter (SSP millions)	2012/13	2013/14	Change	% Increase	2012/13 Share	2013/14 Share
Salaries	2,975	3,568	593	20	45%	37%
Operating	1,391	1,927	536	39	21%	20%
Capital	454	1,791	1,337	295	7%	18%
Transfers	1,816	2,265	449	25	27%	23%
Other	27	182	155.14	575	0%	2%
Total	**6,664**	**9,733**	**3,070**	**46**	**100%**	**100%**

Source: Republic of South Sudan. The Approved National Budget Plan and the Approved Budget 2013/14. Ministry of Finance, Commerce, Investment and Economic Planning. P. 20.

Non-oil revenue continued to increase from 2013/14 to SSP962 million by March 2015. This was less than half the budgeted amounts, falling short a total of SSP1, 692 million. A portion of this shortfall was attributed to the continued decrease in economic activity. Donor grant funding increased slightly from 2013/14 as a result of the enduring crisis, and has been below

---

185   Ibid. p. 20.

budgeted levels.[186]

In line with need to invest in growth and development of South Sudan in the coming years, the President's spending priorities for the 2013/14 fiscal year were as follows[187]:

a. Improving basic services in education, health and water for the people in rural areas.

b. Rapid development of infrastructure to support economic development.

c. Boosting the agriculture and non-oil sectors of the economy to create jobs.[188]

6.4.4. The Budget of the Fiscal Year 2014/15

As regards to 2014/15 revenue and financing plans, total resources for 2014/15 were "estimated to be SSP876 million (8%) higher at SSP11, 279 million, than the SSP10, 403 million budgeted for 2013/14. Net oil revenue was estimated at SSP8, 889 million in 2014/15, a SSP1, 927 million (28%) increase over SSP6, 972 million budgeted for 2013/14. Grant financing was estimated to decline by SSP192 million (55%) in 2014/15 compared to the SSP350 million budgeted for 2014/15. However, grant financing for 2013/14 was not realized. Net financing was estimated to be negative in the amount of SSP433 million, as South Sudan starts to pay down its loans. Actual non-oil revenue collections for 2013/14 were only SSP951 million."[189] In table 6.4 below is the planned

---

186   Source: Republic of South Sudan. The Approved National Budget Plan and the Approved Budget 2013/14. Ministry of Finance, Commerce, Investment and Economic Planning. P. 6.

187   Ibid. p. 20.

188   Ibid. P. 21.

189   Republic of South Sudan, Ministry of Finance and Economic Planning. Approved Budget, Financial Year 2014/15 (August 2014). P. 10.

revenues and financing for the year 2014/15 (SSP Millions).

Net financing from loans for 2014/15 is far higher than projected. Domestic borrowing from the Bank of South Sudan as a result of the monthly overdraft facility totaled SSP6,593 million (principal and interest) by March 31st. Total net financing was equal to SSP4,915 million.

The crisis continued to put pressure on budget execution. As mentioned in the 2014/15 Approved Budget, SSP1 billion of salaries and transfers spending was deferred from 2013/14 fiscal year to the start of 2014/15 fiscal year. In addition, security concerns continued to dominate budget execution.

Table 6.4: Shows the Planned Revenues and Financing for the Fiscal Year 2014/15:

	2013/14 Budget Original	2014/15 Budget Plan	2014/15 Increase Nominal	2014/15 Increase % Change
Net-Oil Revenue	6,972	8,899	1,927	28%
Non-Oil Revenue	1,967	2,654	687	35%
Grants	350	158	-192	-55%
Net Financing	1,114	-433	-1,636	-139%
-new borrowing	4,914	3,278	-1,636	-33%
-loan repayments	3,800	3,711	-89	-2%
Total Resources	**10,403**	**11,279**	**876**	**8%**

Source: Republic of South Sudan, Ministry of Finance and Economic Planning. Approved Budget, Financial Year 2014/15 (August 2014). P. 10.

Pertaining to the 2014/15 expenditure plans, and in line with the increase in the resource envelop total spending was estimated at SSP11, 279 million. This was an increase of SSP876 (8%) in 2014/15 over the SSP10, 403 million in spending budgeted for 2013/14.[190] All the government financed spending increase was to be allocated to an arrears fund to address the backlog of arrears accumulated in previous years and an emergency contingency fund designed to deal with national emergencies. Agency spending was estimated to increase by 2% with funds provided by donors. The planned expenditure for 2014/15 and that in building block are as shown in tables 6.5 and 6.6.

Table 6.5: Shows the Planned Expenditure for the year 2014/15 (SSP Millions)

	2013/14 Budget Original	2014/15 Budget Plan	2014/15 Increase Nominal	2014/15 Increase % Change
Total Resources	**10,403**	**11,279**	**876**	**8%**
Agency Spending	9,733	9,969	236	2%
-Own Resources	9,563	9,532	-31	0%
-External Resources	170	437	267	157%
Arrears Fund	500	800	300	60%
Emergency Contingency Fund	0	250	250	
Interest Payments	170	260	90	53%
Total Expenditures	**10,403**	**11,279**	**876**	**8%**
Surplus/Deficit	**0**	**0**	**0**	

Source: Republic of South Sudan, Ministry of Finance and Economic Planning. Approved Budget, Financial Year 2014/15 (August 2014). P. 11.

---

190   Ibid. P. 10.

The unique situation surrounding the planning and formulation of the 2014/15 budget called for a new strategy, which was provided by the Minister when he presented the "building blocks" strategy to the Council of Ministers and National Legislative Assembly in March 2014. Below is the table showing budget allocations to building blocks.

Table 6.6: Shows 2014/15 Planned Expenditure by "Building Block"

S/No.	Building Block	Allocation (millions)
1	Salaries	4,378
2	Transfers to States and Counties	2,470
3	Basic Operations	2,704
4	Arrears Fund	800
5	Emergency Contingency Fund	250
6	Priority Investments in Peace and Reconstruction	676
	Total	11,279

Source: Republic of South Sudan, Ministry of Finance and Economic Planning. Approved Budget, Financial Year 2014/15 (August 2014).P. 11.

During 2014/15 budget execution, there was a decrease in oil revenues and shortfalls in non-oil revenues against budgeted figures which meant that government revenues fell short of projections up to the end of March 2015 by SSP4,063 million. This has caused deferrals of salary payments as well as reduction in operating expenditure.

Table 6.7: Shows the Summary Budget Execution for the Fiscal Year 2014/15:

In millions SSP	2014/15 Approved Budget	2014/15 July-March Outturns	Variance
Gross Oil Revenue	12,780	5,684	(7,096)
Tariff, transit and TFA payments to Sudan	3,413	1,933	(1,480)
2%/3% for oil producing states/communities	468	91	(377)
Net Oil Revenue	**8,899**	**3,660**	**(5,239)**
PIT	332	271	(61)
Sales tax/VAT	975	204	(771)
Excise	359	139	(220)
Business Profit Tax	209	70	(139)
Customs	116	131	15
Other Revenue (fees, licenses)	663	147	(516)
Non-oil Revenue	**2,654**	**962**	**(1,692)**
Grants from Donors	158	99	(59)
Total Resources	**11,711**	**4,721**	**(3,947)**
Total Spending	**11,279**	**8,826**	**(2,453)**
New Borrowing	3,278	7,225	3,947
Loan Repayments (Principal + Interest)	3,711	2,310	(1,401)
Net Financing	(433)	4,915	5,348
Surplus/Deficit	**(1)**	**810**	**811**

Source: The Republic of South Sudan. The Approved Budget Fiscal Year 2015/16. Ministry of Finance and Economic Planning October 2015. P. 6.

Oil production continued to be lower in the 2014/15 financial year as a result of the enduring crisis, and oil prices declined sharply from October 2015. Lower than expected, payments to Sudan and reduced payments to oil producing communities slightly offset the impact of reduced oil production and prices. Net oil revenues for the first three quarters were SSP3, 015 million below projected levels.

Measures were taken by the Ministry of Finance and Economic Planning to ensure a minimum amount of operating spending to be allocated to the majority of the spending agencies of the Government. In addition to the overdraft facility from the Bank of South Sudan, these measures ensured that funding was available for essential Government expenditure. Salaries for government personnel and transfers to states and counties continued to be paid, though not always within the calendar month. However, these measures have also limited expenditures to recurrent government spending, rather than development expenditure.

Overall, the shortfall in revenues and grants, financed by the Bank of South Sudan loans, presents a challenging context for executing the 2015/16 budget.[191]

6.4.5. The Budget of the Fiscal Year 2015/16

Total resources before financing for 2015/16 were estimated to be significantly lower, at SSP6, 843 million compared to the SSP11, 553 million budgeted for 2014/15. Net oil revenues were estimated at SSP1, 515 million in 2015/16, SSP7, 384 million lower than the net oil revenues estimated for 2014/15. In consultation with the Assembly, non-oil revenues were estimated to increase significantly to SSP5, 328 million in 2015/16. This reflects an ambitious effort to increase non-oil revenue collections.

---

191   The Republic of South Sudan. The Approved Budget Fiscal Year 2015/16. Ministry of Finance and Economic Planning October 2015.P. 7.

Table 6.8: Shows the Projected Revenues and Financing for the Fiscal Year 2015/16

In SSP millions	2014/15 Approved Budget	2014/15 Outturns to March 2015	2015/16 Budget estimates	Nominal change
Net Oil Revenue	8,899	3,660	1,515	(7,384)
Non-Oil Revenue	2,654	962	5,328	(2,674)
Grants from Donors	158	76	128	(30)
Total Resources	11,711	4,698	6,971	(4,740)

Source: The Republic of South Sudan. The Approved Budget Fiscal Year 2015/16.Ministry of Finance and Economic Planning October 2015.P. 11.

Net oil revenues in 2015/16 were forecasted to be SSP7, 384 billion less than projected for 2014/15. The Ministry of Petroleum and Mining and the Ministry of Finance and Economic Planning arrived at a share estimates for oil production and prices. Oil production from Upper Nile was assumed to be an average of 4 million barrels per month throughout the year, with an average government share of 50%. Production in Unity was not assumed to resume during the 2015/16 financial year. The average oil price was conservatively estimated at USD50 per barrel after the Dar blend price discount.

Delays in paying transit and transfer fees to Sudan in 2014/15 resulted in to a series of transfers in kind to Sudan, beginning in the last quarter of the 2014/15 financial year and expected to continue for several months in the 2015/16 fiscal year. These transfers in kind were expected to amount to SSP239 million. During 2015/16 fiscal year, Nile Petroleum was expected to receive SSP312 millions of gross oil revenues, all of which was to be remitted to the government.

Non-oil revenue collection was expected to increase by 300% from current levels due to improvements in collection. Actual non-oil revenue collection for 2014/15 was projected to increase over 40% from 2013/14 outturns. The non-oil revenue estimates therefore reflected ambitious improvements in sales tax and customs revenue collection over the course of the 2015/16 fiscal year.

Grants from donors supporting the GRSS budget were expected to amount to SSP128 million in 2015/16. This represented a 19% decrease from budgeted levels for 2014/15. The ongoing crisis has meant donor grant funding was not expected to increase in 2015/16.[192]

Total spending from government resources for the fiscal year 2015/16 was estimated to be at SSP10, 286 million, representing an SSP555 million (or 6%) decrease against the budgeted levels for 2014/15. Donor funding was estimated to enable a further SSP338 million in externally financed government expenditure.

---

192   Ibid. p. 11.

Table 6.9: Shows the Planned Expenditure for Fiscal Year 2015/16

In SSP millions	2014/15 Approved Budget	2014/15 Outturns to March 2015	2015/16 Budgeted Estimates	Nominal change
Agency Spending (own resources)	9,533	8,541	10,204	671
Arrears Fund	800	2	-	(800)
Emergency Contingency Fund	250	1	-	(250)
Interest Payments	260	170	100	(160)
Externally Funded Spending	436	80	338	(98)
Total Spending	**11,279**	**8,794**	**10642**	**(637)**

Source: The Republic of South Sudan. The Approved Budget Fiscal Year 2015/16. Ministry of Finance and Economic Planning October 2015. P. 12.

The Government of South Sudan recognizes the reality of the current macroeconomic position of South Sudan. Expenditure plans for 2015/16 were based on two principles:[193]

1. Keeping the essential operations and services of the Government of South Sudan running; and

2. Reflect actual current spending better in the national budget.

As such, government expenditure for 2015/16 was concentrated in three of the five chapters, in order of priority: salaries, state transfers and operating expenditure.[194]

---

193   The Republic of South Sudan. The Approved Budget Fiscal Year 2015/16. Ministry of Finance and Economic Planning October 2015. P. 12.

194   Ibid. pp. 12-13.

6.4.5.1. Salaries

The salary chapter budget for 2015/16 was formulated based on the 2015/16 wage bill. Agencies have been provided with budgets for salaries based on the number of staff employed and to be paid by agencies of the Government of South Sudan in 2015/16 fiscal year. The intention was not to reward those agencies that are paying salaries beyond their nominal roll, nor to punish those agencies that have shown fiscal prudence.

This salary budget instead gave the Government of South Sudan a window of opportunity to reform the payroll starting in 2015/16 fiscal year. The salaries budget was a once-off adjustment, not a precedent. There were three reasons for this approach:

1. A number of agencies had recruited in excess of their nominal rolls. This had occurred even despite the hiring freeze instituted in 2012. Not budgeting for these staff members build unbudgeted overspending into the budget, and would have been a misrepresentation of the public finances of South Sudan.

2. Inefficient spending had started to affect the salaries budget execution. Overspending on unbudgeted items was seen also in overtime, incentives, job specific allowances and medical benefits. In some cases such expenditure replaced salaries for staff not (yet) included in the nominal roll.

3. The scale of the problem in the salaries budget was not well known and understood. By outlining the full scale of the problem the Ministry of Finance and Economic Planning took the first step in addressing the problem with the payroll.

In order to regularize and better account for the expenditure on the wages and salaries of the Government of South Sudan, the approach allowed agencies to get their payrolls aligned to their nominal roll based on their then affordable recruitment level. The net effect was a 2015/16 budget for the salaries chapter that was over SSP1 billion higher than 2014/15. To support this measure, the Ministry of Finance and Economic Planning was not any longer to accept pay sheets which were not verified and approved by the Ministry of Public Service and Human Resource Development.

Salaries budget expenditure had grown to over half of the total government spending of the Republic of South Sudan. At the same time, the Government recognized that large numbers of employees and organized forces cannot simply be laid off. The Government of South Sudan was committed to a process of screening the payroll and improving the efficiency of payroll budget execution. The Ministry of Finance and economic Planning and the Ministry of Public Service and Human Resource Development were engaged in a joint effort to do so in the 2015/16 fiscal year.[195]

---

195   Ibid. p. 13.

Table 6.10: Budget Allocations by Chapter
for the Year 2015/16:

In SSP millions	2014/15 Approved Budget	2014/15 Outturns to March 2015	2015/16 Budget estimates	Nominal change
Salaries	4,412	4,326	5,463	1,051
Operating	2,469	1,718	1,672	(797)
Transfers	2,466	1,929	2,795	329
Capital	1,227	451	266	(961)
Other	268	116	108	(160)
Total Expenditures	**10,842**	**8,541**	**10,304**	**(538)**

Source: The Republic of South Sudan. The Approved Budget Fiscal Year 2015/16. Ministry of Finance and Economic Planning October 2015. P. 13.

Donor grant funding for on-budget projects totaled SSP235 million in 2015/16, exceeding the budget of SSP128 million. However, the US dollar value of the grants was only USD26 million, more than USD 15 million below the budget forecast, and USD 5 million lower than the previous year's outturns. However, on-budget funding coordinated with the Government represents a small fraction of total donor funding to South Sudan, which was approximately USD700 million for development projects in 2015/16, and USD1.9 million including humanitarian support.

The continued low level of oil revenues, high inflation and weak economic output presented a significant challenge to budget execution over the course of 2016/17. Tables 6.11 and 6.12 showed that budgeted expenditure for 2016/17 was just going to be 41% of the 2015/16 budget in USD terms. Even then, there was unlikely to be enough cash available to execute all budgeted items. Expenditure was likely needed to be prioritized within the budget ceilings. Even if all budgeted items were executed, the deficit was just going to be 19% of the 2015/16 level in USD terms. This was an extremely austere Budget.

In order to stabilize the economy, it was necessary for there to be three main areas of change. Firstly, Government must implement fiscal and economic reforms. These reforms were aimed at controlling public expenditure; increasing revenues; and encouraging foreign and domestic investment, with an aim to encourage diversification of the economy. Second, peace was to be there as a necessary part of any recovery. Finally, external support was necessary, whilst the foundations of a recovery were to be put in place, to assist in finding expenditure reductions and alleviating poverty. However, international support was likely to be heavily dependent on decisive initial steps towards peace and to correct fiscal imbalances.[196]

6.4.5.2. Transfers

Transfers to state institutions and state level line ministries are essential for providing basic services to all communities of South Sudan. This had remained as a priority of the Government. Despite the fiscal challenges, transfers to the States and Counties increased slightly in the fiscal year 2015/16 from that of the fiscal year 2014/15. Total transfers was to amount to SSP2,795 million, or SSP2,875 million including transfers to oil producing states and communities in Unity and Upper Nile States. Transfers therefore accounted for more than a quarter (27%) of the national budget.

---

196   The Republic of South Sudan, Ministry of Finance and Planning. Approved National Budget Plan and Approved Budget for FY 2016/17. December 2016. P. 14.

Additional allocations were given to the Greater Pibor Administrative Area, totaling SSP141 million. Furthermore, the Ministry of Finance and Economic Planning budgeted for additional transfers to fund the establishment and improvement of basic social services at state and county level, including Primary Health Care Centers and Teacher Training Institutes.[197]

6.4.5.3. Operating and Capital

The Combined salaries and transfers budget for the fiscal year 2015/16 was SSP8,258 million, leaving very little room for spending on operating and capital for the majority of agencies, as has been the case throughout the 2014/15 fiscal year. Measures were taken by the Ministry of Finance and Economic Planning in the 2014/15 fiscal year to ensure a minimum threshold amount of operating funds for all agencies of the Government to enable them to continue operating. The operating budget allocations seek to accurately reflect, first and foremost, the necessary level of operating expenditure to keep the Government of South Sudan operational.

In addition, the Ministry of Finance and Economic Planning allocated further operating funds to those revenue generating agencies to be able to carry out their activities. Additional funds were also provided to those agencies responsible for priority areas as expressed in the Three Year Action Programme, including preparing for the process of holding a national census in 2016/17 and elections in 2017/18.

Meanwhile capital spending was allocated primarily to two sectors: infrastructure and security. The majority of capital budget execution for 2014/15 (over 87%) was concentrated on those two sectors, as reflected in the 2015/16 budget allocations.

---

197   Ibid. p. 13.

A total capital budget of SSP222 million was allocated to these two sectors. Funds for capital expenditure were mainly to go towards the construction, repair and maintenance of roads in the Republic of South Sudan.[198]

Table 6.11: Shows Budget Allocation by Sector from fiscal year 2014/15 to fiscal year 2015/16:

In SSP millions	2014/15 Approved Budget	2014/15 Outturns to March 2015	2015/16 Budget Esti-mates	Nominal change	2015/16 % share of total
Accountability	258	217	272	14	3%
Economic Functions	318	229	237	(81)	2%
Education	604	393	677	73	7%
Health	385	178	316	(69)	3%
Infrastructure	183	130	185	2	2%
Natural Resources and Rural	342	239	361	19	4%
Public Administra-tion	876	888	891	15	9%
Rule of Law	1,546	1,095	1,580	34	15%
Security	3,969	4,379	4,580	611	44%
Social and Humani-tarian Affairs	98	36	92	(6)	1%
Transfers	955	756	1,013	58	10%
Contingencies, Ar-rears and Interest	1,310	173	100	(1,210)	1%
Total Expenditures	10,842	8,714	10,304	(540)	

Source: The Republic of South Sudan. The Approved Budget Fiscal Year 2015/16. Ministry of Finance and Economic Planning October 2015. P. 14.

---

198   Ibid. p. 14.

6.4.6. The Budget of the Fiscal Year 2016/17

Total government spending for the fiscal year 2016/17 was SSP16, 869 million, which was SSP6, 885 million above budget, such that 164% of the annual budget was spent over the fiscal year.

Table 6.12: Shows the Budget Execution for the Fiscal Year 2016/2017:

Particulars	2015/16 Approved Budget	2015/16 Outturns	2016/17 Budget
Gross Oil Revenue	**3,540**	**13,222**	**46,833**
Tariff, Transit and TFA payments	1,706	492	16,161
Transfers in kind to Sudan	239	4,275	21,462
Nile Petroleum payments	0	882	1,512
2%/3% to oil producing states and communities	80	20	461
Net Oil Revenue	**1,515**	**7,553**	**7,238**
Personal Income Tax	1,243	1,138	2,483
Sales Tax/VAT	1,345	897	2,630
Excise	730	378	1,034
Business Profit Tax	334	549	1,295
Customs	740	1,649	1,170
Other Revenue (fees, licenses)	936	287	644
Non-Oil Revenues	**5,328**	**4,899**	**9,256**

Grants from Donors	128	235	2,041
Total Resources	**6,971**	**12,687**	**18,535**
Salaries	5,463	7,487	14,358
Operating	1,672	4,208	5,096
Capital	266	2,099	1,588
Transfers	2,795	2,986	6,321
Other	8	45	38
Peace	0	0	4,500
Interest	100	43	155
Revenue Collection Charges	0	877	0
Total Government Spending	**10,3044**	**17,745**	**33,389**
Externally funded spending	338	658	2,041
Total Spending	**10,642**	**18,403**	**35,429**
Surplus/(Deficit)	**–3,671**	**–5,718**	**–16,894**
New Borrowing	3,671	13,748	11,644
Repayments	0	4,974	7,875
Net Financing	**3,071**	**8,784**	**3,769**

Source: The Republic of South Sudan, Ministry of Finance and Planning. Approved National Budget Plan and Approved Budget for FY 2016/17. December 2016. P. 12.

Table 6.13: Shows the Execution
for the fiscal years 2015/16 and 2016/17

Particulars	2015/16 Approved Budget	2015/16 Outturns	2016/17 Budget	Size of 2016/17 as % of 2015/16 Budget
Gross Oil Revenue	**1,196**	**4,467**	**669**	**56%**
Tariff, Transit and TFA payments	576	166	231	40%
Transfers in kind to Sudan	81	1,444	307	380%
Nile Petroleum payments	-	298	22	-
2%/3% to oil producing states and communities	27	7	7	24%
Net Oil Revenue	512	2,552	103	20%
Personal Income Tax	420	384	35	8%
Sales Tax/VAT	454	303	38	8%
Excise	247	128	15	6%
Business Profit Tax	113	185	19	16%
Customs	250	557	17	7%
Other Revenue (fees, licenses)	316	97	9	3%
Non-Oil Revenues	**1,800**	**1,655**	**132**	**7%**
Grants from Donors	143	79	29	67%
Total Resources	**2,355**	**4,286**	**265**	**11%**

Salaries	1,846	2,529	205	11%
Operating	565	1,422	92	16%
Capital	90	709	23	26%
Transfers	944	1,009	90	10%
Other	3	15	1	33%
Peace	-	-	64	-
Interest	34	15	2	6%
Revenue Collection Charges	-	296	-	-
Total Government Spending	**17,176**	**2,025**	**477**	**41%**
Externally funded spending	114	222	29	26%
Total Spending	**1,215**	**2,100**	**506**	**42%**
Surplus/(Deficit)	**–1,240**	**–1,932**	**–241**	**19%**
New Borrowing	1,240	4,645	166	13%
Repayments	-	1,680	113	-
Net Financing	**1,240**	**2,968**	**54**	**42%**

Source: The Republic of South Sudan, Ministry of Finance and Planning. Approved National Budget Plan and Approved Budget for FY 2016/17. December 2016. P. 13.

Table 6.14: Shows the Detailed Expenditure for the Fiscal Year 2016/17:

	Annual Budget	Q1 Actual	Q2 Actual	Q3 Actual	Q4 Actual	Fiscal Year Actual	Total as % of Budget
Salaries	5,463	1,404	1,429	1,813	2,841	7,487	137%
-Base salaries and pensions	5,264	1,356	1,332	1,452	2,709	6,849	130%
-Incentives, overtime and social benefits	199	48	97	361	132	639	321%
Operating	1,672	556	833	1,970	849	4,208	252%
Capital	266	166	430	1,479	24	2,099	789%
Transfers	2,795	618	692	581	1,095	2,986	107%
Other	8	7	0	38	0	45	586%
Agency Spending	**10,204**	**2,752**	**3,384**	**5,881**	**4,809**	**16,826**	**165%**
Interest	100	9	21	6	7	43	43%
Total Government Spending	**10,304**	**2,761**	**3,405**	**5,888**	**4,816**	**16,869**	**164%**
External Loans	211	2	24	53	345	424	201%
External Grants	128	23	36	51	124	235	183%
Total Spending	**10,643**	**2,785**	**3,465**	**5,992**	**5,285**	**17,528**	**165%**

Source: The Republic of South Sudan, Ministry of Finance and Planning. Approved National Budget Plan and Approved Budget for FY 2016/17. December 2016. P. 15.

6.4.7. The Budget for the Fiscal Year 2017/18

The total estimates of the National Budget for the Fiscal Year 2017/18 amounted to Forty Six Billion Two Hundred and Seventy Six Million Eight Hundred Thirty Thousand Nine Hundred and sixty Eight South Sudanese Pounds only (SSP46, 276,830,968).[199]

In other words, the above total estimated expenditure was referred to as the Resource Envelop for FY 2017/18 budget and is to be realized from the following sources:[200]

1. Net oil revenues of twenty five billion seven hundred and seventy one, four hundred and eighty three thousand, three hundred and thirty two South Sudanese Pounds (SSP25, 771,483,332)…;

2. Non-oil revenues of fourteen billion, forty five million, six hundred and eighty nine thousand, seven hundred and eighty three South Sudanese Pounds (SSP14, 045,689,783);

3. External grants of four hundred and thirteen million, five hundred and thirty three thousand, seven hundred and forty one South Sudanese Pounds (SSP413, 533,741);

4. External project loans of two billion, one hundred and seventy two million, two hundred and ninety three thousand and six hundred and ninety South Sudanese Pounds (SSP2, 172,293,690);

5. Treasury bills of eight hundred and thirty five million South Sudanese Pounds (SSP835, 000,000).

The resource envelop was to be appropriated to cover the expenditures of the following government institutions and obligations:[201]

---

199   Laws of South Sudan. Appropriation Act, 2017/18, September, 2017. P. 3.

200   Ibid. pp. 3-4.

201   Ibid. pp. 3-4.

1. Government spending agencies (Ministries, Commissions, Boards, Corporations, and Others) make payments for salaries to public service employees, use of goods, services costs and capital expenditures;

2. Emergency contingency fund is to cater for national emergencies as a consequence of epidemics, unforeseen acts of nature (floods, drought, famine) or war which could not have been anticipated at the time of preparing the National Budget, and for which spending cannot be postponed without detriment to public interest;

3. Interest payments is for the settlement of loans and borrowings; and

4. Peace budget expenditure is for the purpose of providing for implementation of the Peace Agreement, and the Peace and National Dialogue Committee

6.5. Shocks to South Sudan Economic Environment

The South Sudan economy was hit by a number of negative shocks since independence. The 2012 oil shutdown resulted in a period of austerity which reduced civil servant salaries as well as the scope for development expenditure. The country weathered this period by drawing down on reserves built up during previous periods, and borrowing both domestically and externally. This allowed the government to keep functioning and maintain services. However, as the macro-fiscal situation started to normalize, the outbreak of violence in December 2013 and ensuing hostilities created new fiscal pressures, due to reduced oil revenues and increased spending in the security sector.

The hostilities led to a shutdown of oil production in Unity State and closing of a number of wells in Upper Nile. As a result, oil production in 2014/15 was 40 percent lower than projected in November 2013. The projected production for 2015/16 was reduced by a similar amount. Actual and gross revenues declined roughly proportionally. The decline in revenues was worsened further by dramatic decline in oil prices starting in July 2014. Sales price for Dar Blend fell from USD95 per barrel in July 2014 to around USD40in January 2015. In June 2015 the price obtained was a round USD50-55 per a barrel.

The reduction in oil production and the decline in oil prices have resulted in less revenue for government, and less inflow of dollars to the Bank of South Sudan. Domestic demand for foreign currency, mainly to finance imports and meet external financial commitments (e.g. servicing foreign loans and transfers to Sudan), outstripped supply. The macro-fiscal implications were twofold: a widening fiscal deficit, and a large depreciation in the black market exchange rate[202].

Unlike during the 2012 oil shutdown, reserves were depleted, and sufficient new external loans were not forthcoming. There was little room for reducing overall spending as the military conflict that followed from December 2013 crisis which made it necessary to increase allocations to the security sector. The government financed the deficit through its overdraft with the Bank of South Sudan. As a result the supply of SSP (as measured by the monetary base) increased[203].

The distribution of budget allocations among the sectors had no changes markedly from the 2014/15 budget. Security, Rule of Law and Public Administration remained the largest sectors of expenditure for the Government of South Sudan, together ac-

202   Ibid. p. 7.
203   Ibid. p. 8.

counting for 67% of government expenditure. Aside from these sectors, the education sector's share of the budget increased by SSP74 million to 7% of the budget.

6.6. Exemptions

It has been stipulated in the Financial Act, 2017 that "The Minister of Finance and Economic Planning shall be the sole authority to issue exemption letters."[204] There shall be an exemption from the advance payment of tax for:[205]

1. Humanitarian aid when imported by a bona fide organization as prescribed by regulations;

2. Goods imported by a contractor, or other than a local contractor, in the performance of a contract with the United Nations, the UN Specialized Agencies, or other international or governmental donors to the GRSS;

3. Goods imported by the United Nations, the UN Specialized Agencies, or other governmental donors to the GRSS;

4. Personal goods accompanying a traveler, except goods for resale; and

5. Used household effects of any person intending to take up permanent residence in South Sudan.

However, the National Revenue Authority Act, 2016, had relegated the authority for the exemptions to the Commissioner General as stipulated in NRA Act Section 50 thus: *"Any power, duty or function that, immediately before the coming into force of this Act, was vested in the Minister, Deputy Minister, Undersecretary, or any employee in the Ministry of Finance and Economic*

---

204   Laws of South Sudan. Financial Act, 2017, September, 2017. P. 11
205   Ibid. P. 11.

Planning, by virtue of an act of or any instrument made under an act or under a contract, lease, license or other documents is transferred to the Commissioner General or to the appropriate department of the Authority, as the case may be.''[206]

6.7. Taxes and Fees Levied by the Government of South Sudan

The Government of South Sudan levies different types of taxes and fees as prescribed in table 6.15 below:

Table 6.15: Shows types of taxes and fees levied by the GRSS

S/No.	Type of Fees	Designated Authority
1	Personal Income Tax, Excise and Business Profit Tax	Ministry of Finance and Planning (Taxation Directorate)
2	Custom Duties on Goods	Ministry of Finance and Planning (Customs Directorate)
3	The Control of Imports of Food and Drugs	Food and Drug Control Authority
4	The Registration of Non-Governmental Organizations	Relief and Rehabilitation Commission
5	Companies Operating in the Extraction Sector	Ministry of Mining
6	Security	Criminal Investigation Department
7	Civil Registry, Passports and Immigration Control	Immigration, Nationality and Passport
8	Company Registration	Ministry of Justice
9	Work Permits	Ministry of Labour, Public Service and Human Resources Development
10	Trade Licensing, Certification and the Import of Goods	Ministry of Trade

---

206   Section 50. P. 29.

11	Tourism and Wildlife Conservation	Ministry of Wildlife Conservation and Tourism
12	Telecommunications and Postal Services	Ministry of Telecommunication (National Communication Authority)
13	Civil Aviation	South Sudan Civil Aviation
14	Forestry Production	Ministry of Environment and Forestry
15	Medical Committee Examinations and Certifications	Ministry of Health
16	Registration of Faced Based Organizations	Relief and Rehabilitation Commission (RRC)
17	Information, Broadcasting and Print Media	Ministry of Telecommunication (Media Authority)
18	Provision of Electricity	Electricity Corporation
19	Provision of Water	Urban Water Corporation
20	The Provision of Higher Education	General Education and Instruction
21	The Certification of Investments	Investment Authority
22	The Provision of Judiciary Services	Ministry of Justice
23	The Provision of Measurement and Standardization Services	National Bureau of Standards (NBS)
24	Foreign Affairs Services	Ministry of Foreign Affairs and International Cooperation
25	Registration of Petroleum Companies, petrol Stations, Depot, Gas Depot and Exploration Licenses	Ministry of Petroleum
26	Announcement Radio, Scrolling TV and Jingle advert 1M TV	South Sudan Broadcasting Corporation (SSBC)
27	Ground/Surface Water Use Permit Charges	Water Resources and Irrigation
28	GoSS/NGOs Vehicles, Motor Boat Licensing and Port Service	Ministry of Transport
29	Fees Payable in Suits, Arbitration, Interlocutory Matters, Oaths, Land Registration, Attestation and Others	Judiciary of South Sudan
30	Hotel Rentals (Land Rental)	Prisons Service

Source: Extracted by the author from Laws of South Sudan.
Financial Act, 2017, September, 2017. Pp. 17-87.

It is worth mentioning that the charges are made either as percentages of the value of the goods or in amounts in South Sudanese Pound or US dollar. Percentages charged range from 2%, 4%, 5%, 10%, 20%, 25%, and 50% up to 100% respectively.[207] The amounts charged range from SSP2 up to SSP35.7 million or USD100 up to USD1.9 million[208] (this is in case of annual frequency fees for both cases of high fees charges), depending on the magnitude of the value of goods or services.

---

207   Financial Act, 2017. PP. 26–87.

208   Ibid. pp. 26–87.

Chapter Seven

Public Debt

7.1. Concept of a Public Debt

Debt is an amount of money owed by a person, firm or government/the borrower to a lender. It is an amount of money due and payable, from one person to another. Debt is an amount of money borrowed by one party from another. Debts arise when individuals, etc., spend more than their current income or when they deliberately plan to borrow money to purchase specific goods, services or assets such as houses, financial securities, etc.

Debt is when something, usually money, is owed by one party, the borrower or debtor, to a second party, the lender or creditor. Debt is a deferred payment, or series of payments that is owed in the future, which is what differentiates it from an immediate purchase. The debt may be owed by sovereign state or country, local government, company, or an individual. Commercial debt is generally subject to contractual terms regarding the amount and timing of repayments of principal and interest.[209] Loans, bonds, notes, and mortgages are all types of debt. The term can also be used metaphorically to cover moral obligations and other interactions not based on economic value.[210]

Government debt is also known as public debt, national debt or sovereign debt and is money or credit owed by a central government to creditors within the country as well as to international creditors. Government debt is the stock of outstanding I Owe You (IOUs) issued by the government at any time in the past and not yet repaid.

Public debt is money or credit owed by any level of government on behalf of the citizens; either central government, federal government, municipal government or local government by way of borrowing which must be paid back to the lenders at a future date with interest. It arises out of the government's failure to raise revenue to finance (fund) its expenditure. National debt is the debt incurred by the central government and therefore excludes debts by local governments and public corporations.

Government debt, synonymous to sovereign debt,[211] can be issued either in domestic or foreign currencies. Public debt is the total of all borrowing of a government, minus repayments denominated in a country's home currency.

---

209   Superior Court of Pennsylvania (1894). "Brooke et al versus the City of Philadelphia et al". Weekly Notes of Cases Argued and Determined in the Supreme Court of Pennsylvania, the County Courts of Philadelphia, and the United States District and Circuit Courts for the Eastern District of Pennsylvania. Kay and brother. 34 (18): 348.

210   "debt". Oxford English Dictionary (3rd ed.). Oxford University Press. September 2005.

211   "FT Lexicon" – The Financial Times.

Public debt should not be confused with external debt. External debt is the foreign currency liabilities of both the private and public sector that is to be financed out of foreign exchange earnings.[212]

Government debt also known as public interest, public debt, national debt and sovereign debt is the debt owed by a government.[213]

Government debt can be categorized as internal debt owed to lenders within the country and external debt owed to foreign lenders. Another common division of government debt is by duration until repayment is due. Short term debt is generally considered to be for one year or less, and long term debt is for more than ten years. Medium term debt falls between these two boundaries. A broader definition of government debt may consider all government liabilities, including future pension payments and payments for goods and services which the government has contracted but not yet paid.

Governments create debt by issuing securities, government bonds and bills. Less creditworthy countries sometimes borrow directly from a supranational organization (e.g. the World Bank) or international financial institutions.

When the government borrows, it gives its creditors government securities stating the terms of the loan: the principal being borrowed, the interest rate to be paid on the principal, and the schedule for making the interest payments and principal repayment. The amount of outstanding securities equals the amount

212   Mutamba. Op. cit. p. 272.
213   "Bureau of the Public Debt Homepage". United States Department of the Treasury. Retrieved October 12, 2010. "FAQs: National Debt". United States Department of the Treasury. Archived from the original on October 21, 2010. Retrieved October 12, 2010.

of debt that has not yet been repaid; that amount is called "the government debt."

According to Modern Monetary Theory, public debt is seen as private wealth and interest payments on the debt as private income. The outstanding public debt is an expression of the accumulated previous budget deficits which have added financial assets to the private sector, providing demand for goods and services. Adherents of this school of economic thought argue that the scale of the problem is much less severe than is popularly supposed.[214]

7.2. Types of Public Debts

Types of public debts are as follows:[215]

1. Internal and external public debt: An internal debt is money owed by the government to lenders within a country. An internal public debt therefore means that the government borrows from within the country. This may be in form of direct loans from commercial banks, mutual funds, individuals, companies and sale of bonds and treasury bills. An external debt is money owed by the government to foreign lenders. International Monetary Fund (IMF) defines external debt as "the outstanding amount of actual current liabilities that require payment of principal and/or interest by the debtor at some point in the future that are owed to nonresidents by residents of an economy." An external public debt therefore means that the government borrows from foreign sources like foreign banks, individuals, governments, private

---

214   http://hir.harvard.edu/debt-deficits-and-modern-monetary-theory Debts, Deficits and MMT.

215   Mutamba. Op. cit. pp. 272-273.

firms, foundations and international financial institutions like World Bank and IMF.

2. Short term debts and long term debts: A short term debt is a debt that has to be paid within one year or less than a year. Medium term debts are payable within a period ranging between 2-10 years. Long term debts are paid in a period of more than ten years.

3. Funded debt and unfunded debt: A funded debt is a long term debt whose time repayment is not specified but the borrower continues to service the debt by paying the interest until when he feels he is ready to pay the principal. An unfunded debt is a debt with a specified time of repayment. This may be short term, medium term or long term.

4. Floating debt: This is a short term debt incurred by government by selling treasury bills.

5. Reproductive debt and dead weight debt: A reproductive debt is a debt used for creation of assets and invested in productive ventures like road construction, education and industrial sector. It is able to contribute towards servicing its self and final repayment of the principal. Dead weight debt is a debt used to fund nonproductive ventures and expenditure that do not lead to capital accumulation. For example, a debt incurred to finance a war or to host celebrations.

7.3. Debt Settling

Public debt clearing standards are set by the Bank for International Settlements (BIS). Defaults on public debts are governed by laws, which vary from country to country. The IMF has the power to intervene to prevent anticipated defaults. Smaller authorities such as cities, districts and municipal councils are normally guaranteed by their national government. There are various options that a country may use to settle its international debt obligations. These include:[216]

1. **Surplus Budget**: Raising more revenue from taxation by increasing tax rates and expanding the tax base to create a surplus intended to go towards repaying outstanding debts.

2. **International Liquidity**: The country may use its Special Drawing Rights (SDRs) at the IMF to pay off debts.

3. **Debt Rescheduling**: This involves renegotiating the debt to extend the date of payment.

4. **Repudiation**: Complete refusal by a country to pay debts. A country may decide that it will not pay debts.

5. **Debt Conversion**: This involves borrowing from new low interest rate sources to pay off old debts.

6. **Unrequited Exports**: This involves exporting goods to the lender without expecting any payment and using the value of goods to offset the debt.

7. Use of profits realized from government investments.

8. **Use of Accumulated Reserves**: The government may use its foreign currency reserves to pay off debts.

9. **Debt Cancellation/Debt Relief**: A country negotiates for relief from the lender. Most poor countries are being forgiven debts they owe to rich countries and multinational financial institutions like the World Bank and IMF.

10. Printing more money for payment of internal debts. This however causes inflation.

11. **Dis-investment**: Government may sell off some of its investment for purposes of paying the public debt.

---

216   Ibid. p. 273.

7.4. Causes of Public Debts

The countries that are most affected by external debts are the developing countries. Though developed countries also have debts, they have capacity to pay them back. Causes of public debts are:[217]

1. One of the major causes of external public debts is attributed to colonialism. It is argued that developing countries' debts are partly because of the unjust and unfair transfer of the debts of the colonizing powers to them. On independence, some of these countries inherited debts from the colonial masters at high interest rates. For example, a sum of US$59 billion external public debt was imposed on the newly independent States in 1960. With the additional strain of an interest rate unilaterally at 14% per annum, this debt increased rapidly. Before they had even had time to organize their economies, the new debtors were already burdened with a heavy debt.

2. Most developing countries export primary products. The prices of these products have been constantly falling. The effect of this is that the countries cannot reduce their accumulated debts and at the same time low income makes it necessary for them to incur more new debts to supplement domestically raised revenue to support their budgets.

3. Refinancing loans implies taking on new debts to service the old ones. When old debts become due, most countries borrow afresh to pay. This means that they are not reducing their debt obligations but instead switching from one lender to another.

4. Another cause for large debts in the developing countries is the repatriation of money by the expatriates posted by the

---

217   Ibid. pp. 273-275.

rich lenders themselves or international financial institutions. In fact, a large part of the borrowed money is taken back by the lenders in form of salaries, consultancy fees, and interest. Susan George, in her book titled: '***Debt Boomerang: "How Third World Debt Harms Us All"*** (1992), calculated a net of $418 billion borrowed funds flowed back to the lenders between 1982 and 1990.

5. Loans from the United States government are almost without exception tied to the purchase from the creditor nations. Over 80% of America's foreign aid returns directly through its exports to recipient countries. The prime minister of Malaysia once pointed out that: *"Although Japan provides loans, it takes back with its other hand, as if by magic, almost twice the amount it provides."*

6. Reducing burden of taxation: Most governments resort to borrowing as a way of avoiding high taxes which would reduce savings, discourage work and consumption and even make the government unpopular.

7. Foreign debts are given in foreign currencies which local sources of revenue cannot do. Borrowing from external sources is a source of the scarce foreign exchange.

8. Large sums are realized at ago: Borrowing allows the required funds to be available in lump sum rather than trickle in as is the case with other sources of government revenue like taxation. Urgent spending and large-scale projects can be implemented with certainty. It's difficult to finance large projects like construction of dams and air ports with locally generated revenue.

9. Debt crisis especially in the developing countries arise because of the value of the developing country's currencies depreciating faster due to a wide variety of factors.

7.5 Disadvantages of Borrowing

Despite the evident merits of borrowing as a source of revenue, there are many disadvantages associated with borrowing and they are:[218]

1. High rates of interest: Debts are given at an interest. The rate of interest is often high and this makes the country more indebted than the actual amount received.

2. Creates dependency on the lender by the borrower: Loans are often accompanied by conditionalities that tie the borrower to the lender. For example, some loans are given on condition that all purchases are made from the lending country. In essence, all the money lent is taken back in form of purchases from the lender.

3. The borrower must in certain cases have to accept conditions from the lenders. The IMF and the World Bank, for example, require borrowers to implement certain policies before they qualify to borrow. Structural adjustment advice in the past from the IMF and others, has led to the cut down on important spending such as health, education, in order to help repay loans. This has trickled downward and increased poverty among the population.

4. Excess money supply from external loans may cause inflation.

5. Debt repayment deprives the paying country of foreign currency.

6. Unpredictable source of revenue: This is because sometimes the loan delays, comes in bits or in small amount which cannot really foster development.

7. The debt burden is shifted to future generations that may not

---

218   Ibid. p. 275.

have benefited from the loan.

8. Repatriation of debt amount by technical personnel and purchases leads to increased taxation in future to repay the debts. Borrowing only postpones harsh taxation to a future date because at one time, the debt must be paid.

7.6. The Burden of a Public Debt

The burden of a public debt is the cost of borrowing in monetary and non-monetary terms to the present and future generations.[219]

7.7. Public Debt Sustainability

Sustainable debt level is the level of debt which allows a debtor country to meet its full current and future debt service obligations without resorting to further debt relief or rescheduling, preventing arrears from accumulating, while at the same time allowing the economy to have an acceptable level of economic growth.[220]

Governments usually borrow by issuing securities such as government bonds and treasury bills. Sometimes, less credit worthy countries borrow directly from commercial banks or multinational institutions. Some people consider all government liabilities, including future pension payments and payments for goods and services the government has contracted for but not yet paid, as public debt.

There are various indicators used to measure a country's ability to sustain foreign debts. Each indicator has its own advantages, disadvantages, and suitability to deal with specific cases and

---

219   Ibid. p. 275.

220   Ibid. p. 276.

situations. These indicators are ratios that provide a comparison and show the relationship between two items. These indicators reveal the degree of a country's solvency because they take into account the stock of debt at a certain time in relation to a country's ability to generate resources to repay the debt outstanding balance. The first set of debt burden indicators include:

1. Debt to GDP ratio.
2. Foreign debt to exports ratio.
3. Government debt to current fiscal revenue ratio.

A second set of indicators focuses on the short term liquidity requirements of the country with respect to its debt service obligations. Examples of liquidity indicators include the following:

1. Debt service to GDP ratio.
2. Foreign debt service to exports ratio.
3. Government debt service to current fiscal revenue ratio.

There are many other ratios that can be made to measure the debt burden of a country. The part of the debt that is a burden is the dead weight debt; i.e., borrowed funds financing current spending with no benefit to future generations. Building a hospital is reproductive debt as a service will be provided during the servicing of the debt. The classical example of a dead debt is borrowing money to finance wars.

Chapter Eight

FISCAL POLICY

8.1. Introduction

Fiscal policy is based on the theories of British economist John Maynard Keynes. Also known as Keynesian economics, this theory basically states that governments can influence macroeconomic productivity levels by increasing or decreasing tax levels and public spending. This influence, in turn, curbs inflation increases employment and maintains a healthy value of money. Fiscal policy plays a very important role in managing a country's economy.

Fiscal policy is the deliberate government policy to use spending, taxation and borrowing to influence the level of economic activity. Fiscal policy is the collective term for the taxing and spending actions of governments. It is the means by which a government adjusts its spending levels and tax rates to monitor and influence a nation's economy.

By means of fiscal policy, government influences what takes place in an economy by using its revenue and expenditure. Fiscal policy is the deliberate government policy to use spending, taxation and borrowing to influence the level of economic activity. Fiscal policy is the collective term for the taxing and spending actions of governments. It is the means by which a government adjusts its spending levels and tax rates to monitor and influence a nation's economy.[221]

Fiscal policy is the means by which a government adjusts its spending levels and tax rates to monitor and influence a nation's economy. It is the sister strategy to monetary policy through which a central bank influences a nation's money supply. These two policies are used in various combinations to direct a country's economic goals.

Generally speaking, the aim of most government fiscal policies is to target the total level of spending, the total composition of spending, or both in an economy. The two most widely used means of affecting fiscal policy are changes in government spending policies or in government tax policies.

If a government believes there is no enough business activity in an economy, it can increase the amount of money it spends, often referred to as "stimulus" spending. If there are no enough tax receipts to pay for the spending increases, governments borrow money by issuing debt securities such as government bonds and, in the process, accumulate debt; this is referred to as deficit spending.

By increasing taxes, governments pull money out of the economy and slow business activity. But typically, fiscal policy is used

---

when the government seeks to stimulate the economy. It might lower taxes or offer tax rebates, in an effort to encourage economic growth. Influencing economic outcomes via fiscal policy is one of the core tenets of Keynesian economics.

When a government spends money or changes tax policy, it must choose where to spend or what to tax. In doing so, government fiscal policy can target specific communities, industries, investments, or commodities to either favor or discourage production, and sometimes, its actions based on considerations that are not entirely economic. For this reason, the numerous fiscal policy tools are often hotly debated among economists and political observers.

The government uses any of these tools alone or in combination to achieve stated objectives. The way a specific tool of fiscal policy is used depends on the nature of the problem. For example, when prices are very high, taxation is increased but when prices are very low due to low demand, taxes are reduced.

8.2. Objectives of Fiscal Policy

The objectives of fiscal policy are:

1. **Full Employment**: It is the first and foremost objective of fiscal policy in a developing economy to achieve and maintain full employment in an economy. In such countries, even if full employment is not achieved, the main motto is to avoid unemployment and to achieve a state near to full employment. Therefore, to reduce unemployment and underdevelopment, the state should spend sufficiently on social and economic overheads. These expenditures would help to create more employment opportunities and increase the productive efficiency of the economy.

2. **Price Stability**: There is a general agreement that economic growth and stability are joint objectives for underdeveloped countries. In a developing country, economic instability is manifested in the form of inflation. Prof. Nurske believed that "inflationary pressures are inherent in the process of investment but the way to stop them is not to stop investment. They can be controlled by various other ways of which the chief is the powerful method of fiscal policy."

Therefore, in developing economies, inflation is a permanent phenomenon where there is a tendency to the rise in prices due to expanding trend of public expenditure. As a result of rise in income, aggregate demand exceeds aggregate supply. Capital goods and consumer goods fail to keep pace with rising income.

Thus, this results into inflationary gap. The price rise generated by demand pull reinforced by cost push inflation leads to further widening the gap. The rise in prices raises demand for more wages. This further gives to repeated wage price spirals. If this situation is not effectively controlled, it may turn into hyperinflation.

In short, fiscal policy should try to remove the bottlenecks and structural rigidities which cause in balance in various sectors of the economy. Moreover, it should strengthen physical controls of essential commodities, granting of concessions, subsidies and protection in the economy. In a nutshell, fiscal measures as well as monetary measures go side by side to achieve the objectives of economic growth and stability.

3. **To Accelerate the Rate of Economic Growth**: Primarily, fiscal policy in a developing economy, should aim at achieving an accelerated rate of economic growth. But a high rate

of economic growth cannot be achieved and maintained without stability in the economy. Therefore, fiscal measures such as taxation, public borrowing and deficit financing etc., should be used properly so that production, consumption and distribution may not adversely affect the economy. It should provide the economy as a whole while in turn helps to raise national income and per capita income.

4. **Optimum Allocation of Resources**: Fiscal measures like taxation and public expenditure programmes, can greatly affect the allocation of resources in various occupations and sectors. As it is true, the national income and per capita income of underdeveloped countries is very low. In order to gear the economy, the government can push the growth of social infrastructure through fiscal measures. Public expenditure, subsidies and incentives can favourably influence the allocation of resources in desired channels.

   Tax exemptions and tax concessions may help a lot in attracting resources towards the favoured industries. On the contrary, high taxation may draw away resources in a specific sector. Above all, direct curtailment of consumption and social unproductive investment may be helpful in mobilization of resources and the further check of the inflationary trends in the economy. Sometimes the policy of protection is a useful tool of the growth of some socially desired industries in an underdeveloped country.

5. **Equitable Distribution of Income and Wealth**: It is needless to emphasize the significance of equitable distribution of income and wealth in a growing economy. Generally, inequality in wealth persists in such countries as in the early stages of growth, it concentrates in few hands. It is also be-

cause private ownership dominates the entire structure of the economy. Besides, extreme inequalities create political and social discontentment which further generate economic instability. For this, suitable fiscal policy of the government can be devised to bridge the gap between the incomes of the different sections of the society.

To reduce inequalities and to do distributive justice, the government should invest in those productive channels which incur benefit to low income groups which are helpful in raising their productivity and technology. Therefore, redistributive expenditure should help economic development and economic development should help redistribution.

Thus, well-planned fiscal programme, public expenditure can help development of human capital which in turn possess positive effects on economic distribution. Regional disparities can also be removed by providing incentives to backward regions. A distributive tax policy should be highly progressive and aim at imposing heavy taxation on the richer and exempting poor sections of the community. Similarly, luxurious items, which are consumed by the higher section, may be subject to heavy taxation.

6. **Economic Stability**: Fiscal measures, to a large extent, promote economic stability in the face of short-run international cyclical fluctuations. These fluctuations cause variations in terms of trade, making the most favourable to the developed and unfavourable to the developing countries. So, for the purpose of bringing economic stability, fiscal methods should incorporate built-in-flexibility in the budgetary system so that income and expenditure of the government may automatically provide compensatory effect on the rise or fall of the nation's income.

Therefore, fiscal policy plays a leading role in maintaining economic stability in the face of internal and external forces. The instability caused by external forces is corrected by a policy, popularly known as 'tariff policy' rather than aggregative fiscal policy. In the period of boom, export and import duties should be imposed to minimize the impact of international cyclical fluctuations.

To curb the use of additional purchasing power, heavy import duty on consumer goods and luxury import restrictions are essential. During the period of recession, government should undertake public works programmes through deficit financing. In a nut shell, fiscal policy should be viewed from a larger perspective keeping in view the balanced growth of various sectors of the economy.

7. **Capital Formation and Growth**: Capital assures a central place in any development activity in a country and fiscal policy can be adopted as a crucial tool for the promotion of the highest possible rate of capital formation. A newly developing economy is encompassed by a 'vicious circle of poverty'. Therefore, a balanced growth is needed to breakdown the vicious circle which is only feasible with higher rate of capital formation. Once a country comes out of the clutches of backwardness, it stimulates investment and encourages capital formation.

8. **To Encourage Investment**: Fiscal policy aims at the acceleration of the rate of investment in the public as well as in private sectors of the economy. Fiscal policy, in the first instance, should encourage investment in public sector which in turn effect to increase the volume of investment in those channels which are considered most desirable from the point of view of society.

It should aim at curtailing conspicuous consumption and investments in unproductive channels. In the early stages of economic development, the government must try to build up economic and social overheads such like transport and communication, irrigation, flood control, power, ports, technical training, education, hospitals and school facilities, so that they may provide external economies to induce investment in industrial and agricultural sectors of the economy. These economies will be helpful for widening the size of the market, reducing the cost of production and increasing the social marginal productivity of investment. Here, it must be remembered that projects of social marginal productivity should wisely be selected keeping in view its practical implication.

8.3. Functions of Fiscal Policy

Governments have two main tools in their toolbox for managing the economy: fiscal policy and monetary policy. Monetary policy boils down to letting a central bank manage and regulate the economy by manipulating the interest rates. Fiscal policy takes place at an even higher level, managing government spending and taxation to control the economy. Those effects aren't immediately visible as a rise or drop in the interest rate, but they can affect your business dramatically over the long term.

One of the big functions of fiscal policy is to stabilize the economy on a year-by-year or period-by-period basis. If the economy is sluggish or in crisis, as it was in 2007 and 2008, the government might roll out some combination of spending and tax relief to help get things moving again. That's called a loose or expansionary approach. On the other hand, if the economy is over heated and threatening to cause runaway inflation or a dangerous "bubble" in the markets, the government might cut spending and raise taxes as a means of pulling in the reins. That's referred to as a tight or deflationary policy. In an expansionary stage, you might benefit directly from government contracts or guaranteed loan programmes, or indirectly as money begins to flow into and through your community. In deflationary times you may need to work harder to stay competitive, or to be cautious in your expenditures and acquisitions, depending how much your community and your business sector are affected.

8.3.1. Long-Term Development:

Speeding up a slow economy and slowing down a fast one are both short-term objectives, but they share the same goal in creating a stable framework for long-term growth. If the economy never becomes too hot or too cold, companies like yours can make long-term plans in the secure knowledge that you won't be blindsided by a disastrous economic meltdown. Fiscal policy goes beyond that, though, recognizing that the overall good of the economy sometimes requires action that no business could execute. That includes projects like the Tennessee Valley Authority or the construction of the national system of interstate freeways, which generated almost incalculable long-term benefits. Another example is the space programme of the 1960s and early 1970s, which spanned a remarkable number of new technologies. The government launches these projects with an eye to their long-term value as well as the short-term effects of immediate job creation and economic stimulus.

8.3.2. Allocating and Distributing Resources:

Any national government commands pretty substantial revenues, and that's especially true of the United States. One of the key things fiscal policy tries to do is allocate and distribute those resources in a way that creates the greatest benefit for the economy, and the country, as a whole. A large portion of the government's resources go to defense and national security, for example, which protect every citizen. Some funds might be expended in subsidies, grants or loan guarantees that encourage the growth of businesses or entire industries or sectors of the economy. Others might go to social programmes that help keep low-income citizens solvent and productive, boosting the economy from the bottom rather than the top.

A fourth goal of fiscal policy is full employment, which is closely linked to the other goals. A stable and growing economy generates jobs as a side effect-and high levels of employment mean there are plenty of people with paychecks to spend. That stimulates local economies, which helps companies grow, which in turn creates more employment. This is a good thing for the community and the country as a whole, but it can create an issue for individual employers. In times of full employment, you might find it difficult to recruit and retain enough staff, and wages can rise as a result.

8.4. Stances of Fiscal Policy

There are three stances of fiscal policy and they are:

1. **Neutral fiscal policy** is usually undertaken when an economy is in neither a recession nor a boom. The amount of government deficit spending (the excess not financed by tax revenue) is roughly the same as it has been on average over time, so no changes to it are occurring that would have an effect on the level of economic activity.

2. **Expansionary fiscal policy** involves government spending exceeding tax revenue by more than it has tended to, and is usually undertaken during recessions. An expansionary fiscal policy means increasing aggregate demand through lower taxes and higher government spending. Expansionary fiscal policies encourage more spending, hence increasing aggregate demand and boosting the economy. An expansionary fiscal policy occurs when the government lowers taxes and increases spending; thus expanding output (national income). An increase in government spending or a reduction in taxes shifts the aggregate demand curve to the right. An expansionary fiscal policy will expand the economy's growth.

3. **Contractionary/Restrictive Fiscal Policy**. Contractionary fiscal policy occurs when government deficit spending is lower than usual. This may also be referred to as a deflationary fiscal policy or tight fiscal policy. A contractionary fiscal policy means raising taxes and reducing government expenditure. This is intended to discourage spending and economic activity. Such a policy is adopted for example to reduce inflation.

8.5. Tools of Fiscal Policy:

The two main tools of fiscal policy are:

1. **Taxes:** Taxes influence the economy by determining how much money the government has to spend in certain areas and how much money individuals have to spend. For example, if the government is trying to spur spending among consumers, it can decrease taxes. A cut in taxes provides families with extra money, which the government hopes they will turn around and spend on other goods and services, thus

spurring the economy as a whole.

2. **Spending**: It is used as a tool for fiscal policy to drive government money to certain sectors that need an economic boost. Whoever receives those dollars will have extra money to spend, and as with taxes, the government hopes that money will be spent on other goods and services. The key is finding the right balance and making sure the economy doesn't lean too far either way. Prior to the Great Depression in the 1920s, the U.S. government took a very hands-off approach when it came to setting economic policy. Afterward, the U.S. government decided it needed to play a larger role in determining the direction of the economy.

8.6. Components of Fiscal Policy

There are four key components of Fiscal Policy and are as follows:

1. **Taxation Policy**: The government tries to keep the taxes progressive in nature and with the help of direct and indirect taxes controls the Price stability, control of inflation and distribution of income. Higher the tax; lower is the purchasing power of people and lower is the tax; higher is the purchasing power of the people.

2. **Expenditure Policy**: Expenditure policy of the government deals with revenue and capital expenditures. Capital Expenditures of the government include acquisition of long-term assets, such as facilities or manufacturing equipment etc., which will generate business or additional profits to government. Revenue Expenditures are those expenditures which don't create any productive assets such as interest paid by the Government of India on all the internal and external

loans or pension and salaries of government employees.

3. **Investment and Disinvestment Policy:** Investment and Disinvestment Policy refers to investment in the form of FDI or FII in an economy from outside the country or disinvestment of government holding to public or private shares.

4. **Debt/Surplus Management:** If the government received more than it spends, it is called surplus. If government spends more than income, then it is called deficit. To fund the deficit, the government has to borrow from domestic or foreign sources. It can also print money for deficit financing.

8.7. Role of Fiscal Policy in the Developing Countries

In developed countries, fiscal policy is designed to counter mainly cyclical fluctuations. Fiscal policy is also employed in these countries to reuse the rate of growth of income. Fiscal policy in developing countries, however, has a somewhat different role to play. This is because that though these countries experience economic fluctuations, its nature is different.

Firstly, not only fluctuations occur at a low level of income but also there is no scope for stable growth. Secondly, fluctuations are more prominent in the realm of output and price level rather than output and employment level. Due to the pre-eminence of the agricultural sector in these economies, supply becomes relatively inelastic and unemployment problems become severe. But oscillations in income and price level tend to become more violent. Thirdly, because of the preponderance of the agricultural products in export trade, fluctuations get transmitted from the developed countries to the underdeveloped counterparts. As foreign demand for export is subject to frequent changes, the internal economy cannot remain free from such changes or random oscillations. Finally, the nature of inflation is different in developing countries. In view of these reasons, fiscal policy in poor countries has a special role to play.

Underdeveloped countries are entangled in the vicious circle of poverty. By breaking this impasse, a country can bring higher rate of growth. Thus, rapid economic growth seems to be the fundamental goal of fiscal policy in these countries.

But in the process of economic growth these economies experience inflationary rise in prices since these countries are inflation-sensitive countries. Truly speaking, economic stabilization cannot be separated from economic growth.

Thus, *'growth with stability'* is the most fundamental objective of fiscal policy in developing countries. Thus changes the nature of fiscal policy. In developed countries, fiscal policy becomes merely a compensatory character. But in developing countries, it cannot be a compensatory one.

The main goal of fiscal policy in LDCs should be the increase in capital formation so that the vicious circle of poverty can be destroyed. Economic growth of a country greatly depends on capital accumulation. It is the scarcity of capital that causes underdevelopment.

Thus, by raising the rate of capital formation in these countries, a higher and rapid growth can be brought about. But because of the shyness of private capital in these poor countries, the government fills up the vacuum. Huge public expenditure is incurred to create physical infrastructure. But building up social overhead capital, LDCs can strike a higher growth rate.

Further, capital formation of higher order requires the raising of aggregate saving. It is the fiscal policy that can provide scope for raising community saving.

In other words, fiscal policy has to be tailored in such a way that it cannot only raises overall saving but also lowers down the actual as well as potential consumption. Fiscal policy thus, is an instrument that raises saving and capital formation, thereby resulting in a higher economic growth.

Fiscal policy has also to be employed in such a way that the existing scarce resources get channelized in socially productive sectors. Fiscal policy in these countries aims at diverting resources from unproductive sectors to socially necessary lines of development. In other words, fiscal policy is tied to developmental planning so that a higher economic growth can be achieved.

But fiscal policy is not only directed towards achieving higher economic growth alone. It aims at equitable distribution of income and wealth which is a characteristic of all modern mixed poor economies. Existence of such inequality between the rich and the poor is a great social malaise.

In fact benefits of higher economic growth can never lead to an increase in social welfare unless equality is established. A proper fiscal policy can redistribute income and wealth in a society.

But at the same time it has to be borne in mind that the attainment of goals of higher economic growth and income equality is somewhat paradoxical. In other words, if the economic cries for higher economic growth, income inequality is bound to widen. Or if reduction in inequality is considered to be the primary goal, the goal of rapid economic growth will have to be sacrificed to some extent. Hence, the paradox.

But the logic of this point is questionable. In fact, what is required is the conciliation of these two apparently contradictory goals. If well-balanced fiscal instruments are employed, a satisfactory reconciliation between the two fiscal goals of higher economic growth and income equality and, hence, maximum social welfare, is not difficult to achieve.

Finally, fiscal policy has an additional role to play in LDCs which are inflation sensitive countries. In the process of economic growth, inflation is bound to appear in these economies.

Fiscal policy, thus, has to be employed in such a way that a reasonable economic stability can be maintained, but not at the cost of the goal of higher economic growth.

Growth-cum-stability seems to be the most important fiscal objective in developing economies.

8.8. Challenges of Implementing Fiscal Policy

The government has two tools to implement its fiscal policy, namely, taxes and government spending. If the economy is in recession, the government may decide to increase aggregate demand, or decrease taxes to stimulate the economy and increase aggregate demand. Similarly, if the economy is facing inflationary economic boom, it may decrease spending or increase taxes.

When government takes specific actions to influence aggregate demand, it's called the discretionary fiscal policy. The discretionary fiscal policy does not always work as intended by the government. There are many reasons as to why the fiscal policy may not be as effective as desired, or sometimes even be counterproductive. Some of these reasons are discussed below:

1. If the government relies on inaccurate statistics, it's likely to make wrong policy decisions in the first place.
2. There could be a lag in implementing a policy decision, and/ or the impact of a policy decision. For example, by the time the policy makers recognize the problem and take decision to do something, it may already be too late (Recognition lag

and action lag). Once the government implements a policy, there may be a time lag till the policy has an impact on the economy (impact lag).

3. An expansionary fiscal policy may end up decreasing aggregate demand because of crowding-out effect. Increased government borrowing leads to an increase in interest rates, which leads to a decrease in aggregate demand.

4. The economy may be slow because of shortage of resources rather than lower demand. In this case, fiscal policy will not help (it may actually increase inflation).

5. Since expansionary fiscal policy increases fiscal deficit, there is constraint over how much deficit the government can tolerate.

6. While fiscal policy solves one problem, it may aggravate another problem.

8.9. Limitations of Fiscal Policy

Although fiscal policy gained prominence during world depression of 1930's, yet its practical application has a number of problems or limitations. In view of such a situation, let us understand fully the problems and limitations which are associated with a fiscal policy. Some of the major limitations of fiscal policy are as follows:

1. **Policy Lags**: During the recent times, there is no much argument about the desirability or otherwise of a discretionary fiscal policy. The burning question in this context is related with the timing of the fiscal measures. Unless the variation in taxes and public expenditure are neatly timed, the desired counter-cyclical effects cannot be realized.

There is generally some interval between the time when a

particular action is needed and the time when a fiscal measure has its impact felt. The duration of this interval determines the extent to which a specific fiscal measure can be effective. This time interval comprises of three types of lags-recognition lag, administrative lag and operational lag.

(a) **Recognition Lag**: This is the interval between the times when action is needed. This lag may exist when a change in the economy and a report concerning the change do not coincide. Such a lag has duration of three months. It can be reduced if the forecasting is satisfactorily.

(b) **Administrative Lag**: This is the interval between the time when need of action is recognized and the time when the action is actually taken. This is perhaps the most difficult lag to deal with. Even when the need of action has been recognized, the sanction from the legislature and executive must take some time and that may involve about one to five months of time.

In order to reduce such a lag to minimize the legislative and executive red-taps, it is important to keep a shelf of public works in readiness. The recognition and administrative lags together determine the inside lag of fiscal policy and its length, according to Willes, is four to eighteen months.

(c) **Operational Lag**: The time interval between when action is taken and when it has its impact on income and employment is known as the operational or the outside lag. Albert Ando and E. C. Brown have pointed out that the change in personal income and taxes produce significant changes in disposable money income and consumption within a month or two, changes in the corporate tax structure produce changes in corporate spending in about three or four months. Willes was of the view that the outside of fiscal policy has a short duration of one to three months only. J. G. Ranlett, however, considers that these estimates need modification.

2. **Forecasting Lags:** Another most serious limitation of fiscal policy is the practical difficulty of observing the coming events of economic instability. Unless they are correctly observed the amount of revenue to be raised, the amount of expenditure to be incurred or the nature and extent of the budget balance to be framed cannot be suitably planned. In fact, success of fiscal measures depends on the accurate predictions of various economic activities. In its absence, it proves to be a little bit erratic.

3. **Correct Size and nature of Fiscal Policy:** The most important necessity on which the success of fiscal policy will depend is the ability of public authority to frame the correct size and nature of fiscal policy on the one hand, and to foresee the correct timing of its application on the other. It is, however, too much to expect that the government would be able to correctly determine the size, nature of composition and appropriate execution-time of fiscal policy.

4. **Fiscal Selectivity:** When monetary policy is general in nature and impersonal in impact, the fiscal policy, in contrast, is selective. The former permits the market mechanism to operate smoothly. The latter, on the contrary, encroaches directly upon the market mechanism and gives rise to an allocation of resources which may be construed as good or bad depending upon one's value judgments. A particular set of fiscal measures may have an excessively harsh impact upon

certain sectors, while leaving others almost unaffected.

5. **Inadequacy of Fiscal Measures:** In anti-depression fiscal policy, the expansion of public spending and reduction on taxes are always important elements. The question arises naturally, whether a specific variation in public spending or taxes will bear the desired results or not. In case the injections or withdrawals from the circular flow are more or less than what are required, the system will fail to move in the desired direction. This results in exaggeration of instability in the economy.

6. **Adverse Effect on Redistribution on Income:** It is felt that fiscal policy measures redistribute income, the actual effect will be uncertain. If income is redistributed in favour of the low-income classes whose marginal propensity to consume is high, the effect will be increase in total demand. But the fiscal action will be contractionary if large part of the additional income goes to people having higher marginal propensity to save.

7. **Self-Offsetting Effect**: The compensatory fiscal policies of the government may discourage private investment, since the private entrepreneurs have to face a competition from public enterprises in securing labour, raw materials and finances. Moreover, increase involvement of the government in economic activity at the onset of recession strengthens the pessimistic expectations of the private entrepreneurs. The expansion of public spending may be associated with curtailment of private spending. Consequently, the fiscal measures may be self-offsetting.

8. **Reduction in National Income**: Balanced budget multiplier as a fiscal weapon can be gainfully applied during de-

pression is conditioned by the fact of marginal propensity to spend of the recipients of public expenditure being larger than or at least, equal to that of the taxpayers. In case it becomes smaller than the taxpayers, the fiscal programmes under balanced budget will bring about reduction in the national income.

9. **Solution for Unemployment**: The purpose of fiscal policy will be defeated if the policy cannot maintain a rising supply level of work effort. The money of national income will rise with increase in productive efficiency and increased supply of work effort. But if the tax measures are stringent and too high, they will certainly affect the incentive work. This is an important limitation of fiscal policy.

10. **Adverse Effect of Debt Management**: The use of fiscal instruments during unemployment and depression is often associated with the subsequent problem of debt management. Because deficit budgeting is the normal fiscal cure, public debt is made for financing it. And if the process of recovery from depression is long, the creation of budget deficit year after year will create a huge problem of debt repayment and debt management.

11. **Adverse Psychological Reaction**: Large deficit programmes financed by borrowing bring about adverse psychological reactions. Rumours of government bankruptcy discourage investors and often flight of capital takes place.

12. **Hardships in Under Developed Countries:** The creation of additional income through compensatory fiscal measures is not easily possible in underdeveloped countries as in advanced economies. This is mainly because a stagnating agricultural sector dominates the largest part of their economy

where marginal propensity to consume is so high that most of the additional income is consumed and the marketable surplus is the least.

13. **Administrative Problems in Democratic Countries:** In a democracy, fiscal policy measures must be a time-consuming process. Legislative actions, administrative tasks, and the executive process are often delayed and the original estimates of revenue earnings and government expenditures often become irrelevant. The operational lag relating to fiscal measures results in a considerable erosion of effect and the gap between expected achievement and the real attainment often becomes vast.

8.10. Instruments of Fiscal Policy

Some major instruments of fiscal policy are: Budget, Taxation, Public Expenditure, Public Works and Public Debt.

1. **Budget**: The budget of a nation is a useful instrument to assess the fluctuations in an economy. Different budgetary principles have been formulated by the economists, prominently known as: annual balanced budget, cyclical balanced budget and fully managed compensatory budget.

    a) Annual Balanced Budget: The classical economists propounded the principle of annually balanced budget. They defended it with force till the deep rooted crisis of 1930's. The reasons for their acceptance of this principle are:

    (i) They maintained that there should be a balance in income and expenditure of the government.

    (ii) They felt that automatic system is capable to correct the evils.

(iii) Balanced budget will not lead to depression or boom in the economy.

(iv) It is politically desirable as it checks extravagant spending of the state.

(v) This type of budget assures full employment without inflation.

(vi) The principle is based on the notion that government should increase the taxes to get more money and reduce expenditure to make the budget balanced.

However, this principle is subject to certain objections. These objections are as under:

(i) Classical version that balanced budget is neutral is not well based. In practice, a balanced budget can be expansionary.

(ii) The assumptions of full employment and automatic adjustment are too untenable in a modern economy.

(iii) Some economists also argue that annually balanced budget involves lesser burden of taxes.

(b) **Cyclical Balanced Budget**: The cyclical balanced budget is termed as the "Swedish Budget". Such a budget implies budgetary surpluses in prosperous period and employing the surplus revenue receipts for the retirement of public debt. During the period of recession, deficit budgets are prepared in such a manner that the budget surpluses during the earlier period of inflation are balanced with deficit. The excess of public expenditure over revenues are financed through public borrowings. The cyclical balanced budget can stabilize the level of business activity. During inflation and prosperity, excessive spending activities are curbed with budgetary surpluses while budgetary deficits during recession with raising extra purchase power. This policy is favoured on the following account:

(i) The government can easily adjust its finances according to the needs.

(ii) This policy works smoothly in all times like depression, inflation, boom and recession.

(iii) Cyclical balanced budget simply ensures stability but gives no guarantee that the system will get stabilized at the level of full employment.

(c) **Fully Managed Compensatory Budget**: This policy implies a deliberate adjustment in taxes, expenditures, revenues and public borrowings with the motto of achieving full employment without inflation. It assigns only a secondary role to the budgetary balance. It lays down the emphasis on maintenance of full employment and stability in the price level. With this principle, the growth of public debt and the problem of interest payment can be easily avoided. Thus, the principle is also called 'functional finance'.

The fully managed compensatory budget has been criticized on the following grounds:

(i) It considers that the government should give blanket guarantee against unemployment.

(ii) This policy is not automatic.

(iii) It brings political upheavals as it delays the implementation of appropriate fiscal measures.

(iv) A country is burdened with debt in the long run period.

(v) This policy is a prolonged lag which in practice has a disturbing effect on economy.

2. **Taxation**: Taxation is a powerful instrument of fiscal policy in the hands of public authorities which greatly affect the changes in disposable income, consumption and investment. An anti-depression tax policy increases disposable income of the individual, promotes consumption and investment. Obviously, there will be more funds with the people for consumption and investment purposes at the time of tax reduction. This will ultimately result in the increase in spending activities i.e. it will tend to increase effective demand and reduce the deflationary gap. In this regard, sometimes it is suggested to reduce the rates of commodity taxes like excise duties, sales tax and import duty. As a result of those tax concessions, consumption is promoted. Economists like the Hansen and Musgrave, with their eyes on raising private investment, have emphasized upon the reduction in corporate and personal income taxation to overcome contradictory tendencies in the economy.

Now, a vital question arises about the extent to which unemployment is reduced or mitigated if a tax reduction stimulates consumption and investment expenditure. In such a case, reduction of unemployment is very small. If such a policy of tax reduction is repeated, then consumers and investors both are likely to postpone their spending in anticipation of further fall in taxes. Furthermore, it will create other complications in the government budget.

3. **Anti-Inflationary Tax Policy:** An anti-inflationary tax policy, on the contrary, must be directed to plug the inflationary gap. During inflation, fiscal authorities should not retain the existing tax structure but also evolve such measures (new taxes) to wipe off the existing purchasing power and

consumer demand. To this end, expenditure tax and excise duty can be raised.

The burden of taxation may be raised to the extent which may not retard new investment. A steeply progressive personal income tax and tax on windfall gains is highly effective to curb the abnormal inflationary pressures. Export should be restricted and imports of essential commodities should be liberated.

The increased inflow of supplies from origin countries will have a moderate impact upon general prices. The tax structure may impose heavy burden on higher income group and vice versa. Therefore, proper care must be taken that the government policies should not bring violent fluctuations and impede economic growth. To sum up, despite certain short-comings of taxation, its significance as an effective anti-cyclical and growth inducing investment cannot be forfeited.

4. **Public Expenditure**: The active participation of the government in economic activity has brought public spending to the front like among the fiscal tools. The appropriate variation in public expenditure can have more direct effect upon the level of economic activity than even taxes. The increased public spending will have a multiple effect upon income, output and employment exactly in the same way as increased investment has its effect on them. Similarly, a reduction in public spending can reduce the level of economic activity through the reverse operation of the government expenditure multiplier.

    (i) **Public Expenditure Inflation**: During the period of inflation, the basic reason of the inflationary pressures is excessive aggregate spending. Both private consumption and investment spending are abnormally high. In those circumstances, public spending policy must aim at reducing the government spending. In other words, some schemes should be abandoned and others be postponed. It should be carefully noted that government spending which is of productive nature, should not be shelved, since that may aggravate the inflationary dangers further. However, reduction in unproductive channels may prove helpful to curb inflationary pressures in the economy. But such a decision is really difficult from economic and political point of view. It is true, yet the fiscal authority can vary its expenditure to overcome inflationary pressures to some extent.

(ii) **Public Expenditure in Depression**: In depression, public spending emerges with greater significance. It is helpful to lift the economy out of the morass of stagnation. In this period, deficiency of demand is the result of sluggish private consumption and the investment expenditure. Therefore, it can be met through the additional doses of public expenditure equivalent to the deflationary gap. The multiplier and acceleration effect of public spending will neutralized the depressing effect of lower private spending's and stimulate the path recovery.

5. **Public Works**: Keynes General Theory highlighted public works programme as the most significant anti-depression device. There are two forms of expenditure i.e. Public Works and Transfer Payments.

Public works according to Prof. J. M. Clark are durable goods, and primarily fixed structure, produced by the government. They include expenditures on public works as roads, rail tracks, schools, parks, buildings, airports, post offices, hospitals, irrigation canals etc.

Transfer payments are the payments such like interest on public debt, subsidy, pension, relief payment, unemployment, insurance and social security benefits etc. The expenditure on capital assets (public works) is called capital expenditure.

Keynes has strong faith in such a programme that he went to the extent of saying that even completely unproductive projects like the digging up of holes and filling them up are fully admissible.

Public works are supported as an anti-depression device on the following grounds:

(i)   They absorb hitherto unemployed workers.

(ii) They increase the purchasing power of the community and thereby stimulate the demand for consumption goods.

(iii) They help to create economically and socially useful capital assets as roads, canals, power plants, buildings, irrigation, training centres and public parks etc.

(iv) They provide a strong incentive for the growth of industries which are generally hit by the state of depression.

(v)   They help to maintain the moral and self-respect of the work force and make use of the skill of unemployed people.

(vi) The public works do not have an offsetting effect upon private investment because these are started at a time when private investment is not forthcoming.

The above stated points are, therefore, the evidence that public works programme fully satisfies the main criteria as laid down for public expenditure. However, this form of public expenditure is subject to certain limitations and practical difficulties. Some of these limitations are listed as under:

1. **Difficult Forecasting**: The effectiveness of public works programmes always rests upon accurate forecasting of the depression or boom. But prediction of accurate forecasting is very difficult.

2. **Timing of Public Works**: Another serious problem relates to the timing of public works with the moment of cycle. Due to lack of forecasting, proper timing is neither feasible nor possible. Thus this factor along undermines the significance of public works as an instrument of stabilization.

3. **Delay in Starting**: Public works programmes are not something which can be started immediately. Actually, it is a long term programme which requires proper planning with regard to the finance and engineering. In this way, delay is the natural cause. Dernburg and McDongal have rightly noticed, "public works are, in short, clumsy and slow moving requiring time to get ready and time to turn off."

4. **Scarcity of Resources**: The undertaking of public works programme may pose a serious threat due to non-availability of resources. It is likely that scarcity of resources may further aggravate the crisis instead of giving the pace of smoothness.

5. **Limited Scope of Employment**: The public works programme is not capable of assuring job to all cadres of unemployed workers. Such works are only started to absorb unskilled and semi-skilled workers and not the specialized.

6. **Misallocation of Resources**: As the slump gets deepened, there is widespread unemployment of manpower and equipment. Generally, public works are located in only few selected areas. Thus, they may prove to be inadequate to cope with requirements. Again, immobility in factors of production may also prevent the economic utilization of available

resources. As a result, they reduce the efficiency of public works programme.

7. **Burden of Public Debt**: The public works programme, generally, are financed through borrowing during depression. This will saddle the country with a heavy burden of repayment of principle amount and interest therein.

8. **Cost Price Maladjustments**: The public works programme may perpetuate cost price maladjustments in heavy industries where public expenditure is concentrated. During the period of boom, wages and prices in construction industries have a strong upward tendency while in recession or depression; prices move downward, wages and costs remain sticky relatively. In short, such distortion in cost price structure brings more instability in the economy.

9. **Effect of Private Enterprise**: In certain areas, the construction programmes undertaken by public agencies may compete with private investment. As a result, the latter is driven out of business. In such a case, public works will prove to be self-off setting and aggregate demand will possibly fail to increase.

10. **Control over Public Works**: The success of public works mostly depends on the nature of control over them. If public works are controlled by the central authority, delay is likely to arise in selected projects.

11. **Political Considerations:** Public works are often started in democratic countries in certain areas not on account of economic reasons but the political pressures at national; state and local levels sway the government decisions. Consequently, the economic utility of such public works remains very limited.

6. **Public Debt:** Public debt is a sound fiscal weapon to fight against inflation and deflation. It brings about economic stability and full employment in an economy. The government borrowing may assume any of the following forms mentioned as under:

(a) **Borrowing from Non-Bank Public**: When the government borrows from non-bank public through sale of bonds, money may flow either out of consumption or saving or private investment or hoarding. As a result, the effect of debt operations on national income will vary from situation to situation. If the bond selling schemes of the government is attractive, the people induce to curtail their consumption; the borrowings are likely to be non-inflationary.

When the money for the purchase of bonds flows from already existing savings, the borrowing may again be non-inflationary. Has the government not been borrowing, these funds would have been useful for private investment, with the result that the debt operations by the government will simply bring about a diversion of funds from one channel of spending to another with the similar quantitative effects on national income.

If the government bonds are purchased by non-bank individuals and institutions by drawing upon their hoarded money, there will be net addition to the circular flow of spending. Consequently, the inflationary pressures are likely to be created. But funds from this source are not commonly available in larger quantity. Its main implication is the borrowing from the non-bank public is more advantageous in an inflationary period and undesirable in a depression phase. In short, the borrowing from non-bank public are not of much significant magnitude whether it comes out of consumption, saving, private investment or hoarding.

(b) **Borrowing from Banking System**: The government may also borrow from the banking institutions. During the period of depression, such borrowings are highly effective. In this period, banks have excessive cash reserves and the private business community is not willing to borrow from banks since they consider it unprofitable.

When unused cash lying with banks is lent out to government, it causes a net addition to the circular flow and tends to raise national income and employment. Therefore, borrowing from banking institution has desirable and favourable effect especially in the period of depression when the borrowed money is spend on public works programmes.

On the contrary, borrowing from this source dry up almost completely in times of brisk business activities i.e. boom. Actually, demand is very high during inflation period, since profit expectation is high in business. The banks, being already loaded up and having no excess cash reserves find it difficult to lend to the government. If it is done, it is only through reducing their loans somewhere else. This leads to a fall in private investment. As the government spending is off-set by reduction in private investment, there will be no net effect upon national income and employment.

In a nut shell, borrowing from banking institutions have desirable effect only in depression and is undesirable or with a neutral effect during inflation period.

(c) **Drawing from Treasury**: The government may draw upon the cash balances held in the treasury for financing budgetary deficit. It demonstrates dishoarding resulting in a net addition in the supply of money. It is likely to be inflationary in nature. But, generally, there are small balances over and above what is required for normal day to day requirements. Thus, such borrowings from the treasury do not have any significant result.

(d) **Printing of Money**: Printing of money i.e. deficit financing is another method of public expenditure for mobilizing additional resources in the hands of government. As new money is printed, it results in a net addition to the circular flow. Thus, this form of public borrowing is said to be highly inflationary.

Deficit financing has a desirable effect during depression as it helps to raise the level of income and employment but objection is often raised against its use at the time of inflation or boom. Here it must be added that through this device, the government not only gets additional resources at minimum cost but can also create appropriate monetary effects like low interest rates and easy money supply and consequently economic system is likely to register a quick revival.

Chapter Nine

TAXATION IN

THE REPUBLIC OF SOUTH SUDAN

9.1. Background of Taxation in South Sudan

Public revenues in South Sudan can be traced back to colonial administration. The colonial system imposed social service tax on adult males. Other revenues were generated through imposition of penalties, fines, etc. as local government revenue in 1950s when the country was under Khartoum Government. The social service tax was revenue collected to ensure provision of law and order.

9.2. Administration of Taxation in South Sudan

In accordance with the Taxation Act, 2009, The Director General of the Directorate of Taxation have an exclusive responsibility and authority for the operation and administration of all aspects of the tax system of the Government of the Republic of South Sudan including, but not limited to the implementation of the Taxation Act, 2009, unless otherwise specified. The Director General of the Directorate of Taxation is responsible for providing procedural and other guidance necessary for the collection and remittance of all revenues within South Sudan. The Directorate of Taxation falls under the National Ministry of Finance and Economic Planning.

Directorate of Taxation collects the revenue at the national level. Whereas at the states level, it is the Department of Taxation under the state Ministry of Finance, Trade and Industry which is responsible for taxation issues and is the department that collects the revenue at the state government level. At the Local Government level, it is the Counties that handle taxation. The Commissioner of the county oversees the collection of taxes under the supervision of the Executive Director and Payam Administrators.

The major taxes in the Republic of South Sudan are:[222]

1. Personal Income Tax (PIT).
2. Business Profit Tax (BPT).
3. Value Added Tax (VAT) is now Sales Tax.
4. Excise Tax.
5. Stamp Duty (collected at the state government level).

---

222   Interview with Late John Joseph Ucin, Assistant Director for Large Taxpayers Unit, Taxation Office, Nimra Talata, Juba.

When comparing the revenue generated through the collection of direct taxes and indirect taxes, direct taxes generate more revenue than indirect taxes. There are two rates imposed when collecting direct taxes, particularly the personal income tax. Income form 0-5,000 is charged at the rate of 10% and that of income more than 5,000 is charged at the rate of 15%.[223]

9.3. Departments of Taxation Administration

Tax Administration of South Sudan consists of the following departments:

1. Tax Operations Department
2. Administration and Finance Department

1. **Tax Operations Department**

This department has two units:

   a. Operation Unit.
   b. Policy and Procedures and Research and Coordination Unit.

Tax Operation in the Headquarters is divided into two for the purpose of management and simple supervision as follows:

   i. Large Taxpayers Unit (LTU): It was established in August 2012 and is responsible for collection of taxes from large tax payers such as large companies.[224]

   ii. Small and Medium Taxpayers Unit (SMTU). Is responsible for collection of taxes from small and medium companies.

---

223   Interview with Late John Joseph Ucin, Assistant Director for Large Taxpayers Unit, Taxation Office, Nimra Talata, Juba.

224   Ibid.

There are four functional subunits under each unit such are (Taxpayer Service, Collection, Return Processing and Revenue Reconciliation and tax Audit and Investigation).

In 2010, Tax Administration established an Electronic System called Directorate of Taxation Information System (DTIS). It was set in accordance with provisions of Taxation Act, 2009 as amended to date with support from USAID through Deloitte Consultancy. It's a unique system that can generate TIN Numbers to the taxpayers and manage Taxpayers Accounts' (processing the payments, returns and other necessary functions).

There are taxation offices in the former ten states collecting national taxes revenue, two offices are not functioning, Malakal and Bentiu the former Unity State due to 2013 conflict in the country.

2. Administration and Finance Department

It is the department that deals with Human resources (personnel) and procurement issues, and processing accounts and payments connected with the whole Directorate of Taxation.

9.4. Direct Taxes Rates in South Sudan

The major examples of direct taxes are personal income tax and business profit tax.

Direct taxes are imposed at the rates shown in tables 9.1 and 9.2 opposite:

Table 9.1: Shows Income Tax Rates

No.	Amount of taxable income per month	Tax Rate
1.	300SSP	Not subject to income tax (zero rate)
2.	301SSP-5,000SSP	10% (ten percent)
3.	5,001 and above	15% (fifteen percent)

Table 9.2: Business Profit Tax Rates are as in the table below:

No.	Types of Business	Tax Rate
1.	Small businesses	10% (ten percent)
2.	Medium businesses	15% (fifteen percent)
3.	Large companies	20% (twenty percent)

It is worthy to mention that the rates of direct taxes in the two tables above signify progressive tax rates for income tax and business profit tax. Progressive tax rate is also applied for indirect taxes as in table 9.3 where excise tax for insurance companies is 10% and that for airlines companies are 15%.

9.5. Challenges in the Tax Administration

The challenges faced by tax Administration in carrying out its task were as below:

1. The tax system of South Sudan is based on policy of self-assessment which allowed the taxpayers to assess their tax liabilities and pay to the Directorate of Taxation. Taxpayers usually understated the taxes and pay less. The support to

this policy is audit and investigations functions to promote taxpayers compliance, but currently the audit activities have been suspended in April 30th, 2018, and in the absence of audit activities the Directorate faced two challenges of non-compliance and underestimation of the tax liabilities by tax-payers.

2. Lack of skilled staff is still one of the major challenges in tax administration.
3. Taxation offices outside Juba are not connected to the DTIS.
4. Previous exemptions are still existing which has a direct im-pact on the nonoil revenue collection performance despite IMF recommendations for the setting up the exemptions committee in the Ministry of Finance to advise the Minister.
5. Lack of vehicles for field visits and getting staff to work.
6. Costly maintenance of old vehicles results into spending of 80% of the operation cost.
7. Lack of generator services for the office.
8. Lack of office maintenance.
9. Fuel shortages at most times.
10. Lack of funds for taxpayers' education to publish brochures; hold seminars and media results in high level of non-com-pliance taxpayers.
11. Lack of support to enforce laws for tax evasion.
12. Lack of internet within the Directorate of Taxation had im-pacted access to tax information.
13. No set between the bank and DTIS to reflect taxpayer pay-ments on time.
14. Huge tax return backlogs due to lack of computers and lack of training.
15. Lack of own accommodation to maximize use of net-weak server.

16. Lack of IT specialist in the Tax Administration to monitor functioning of DTIS.
17. Lack of adequate incentives for tax officials creates low morale, temptations and corruption practices.
18. Delays of salaries cause so many absentia and disobedience.
19. Ministry of Finance and Planning appointment of unqualified and inexperienced tax officials without consultation with the Directorate of Taxation authorities.

9.6. Measures Taken to Improve Revenue Collection in Tax Administration

The measures taken to improve the collection of revenue were as follows:

1. Implementation of the amendment of Taxation Act, 2016 and Financial act, 2017/18 which imposed new taxes and rates.
2. Increment of excise duty on alcohol and tobacco products.
3. Imposed 20% withholding tax on government contracts.
4. Imposed 15% withholding on technical fees for professionals.
5. Increased rental tax from 10% to 20%.
6. Revising the exemption criteria.

9.7. The Way Forward to Overcome the Challenges

1. Improve revenue reconciliation and accounting, and updating taxpayers' ledgers through training.
2. Taxpayers' education and awareness about their tax obligations and responsibilities especially with the new changes in the Tax laws through workshops and media.
3. Introduce revenue collection through banks in the states national taxation offices for efficient management of the taxes revenue.

4. Implementation of National Revenue Authority to stop all activities of collection of unauthorized taxes by the States Revenue Authorities.
5. Appointing the permanent IT specialist to monitor DTIS functions.
6. NRA is expected to bring a number of benefits and diffuse challenges such as:
   a. Addressing the issue regarding the workforce.
   b. Provide a framework for better cooperation, coordination and information exchange across the revenue institutions.
   c. Delays to establishing functional NRA that creates too much anxiety.

9.8. Indirect Taxes Rates in South Sudan

Table 9.3: Rates of Leading Indirect Taxes

No.	Types of leading indirect taxes	Tax Rate
1.	**Excise tax**: Insurance Companies Air Lines Companies	 5% (five percent) 10% (ten percent)
2.	**Sales tax**	15% (fifteen percent) during the period of austerity measures but before that it was 5% (five percent)

There is a contrary view that indirect taxes generate more revenue than direct taxes because there are many sources of indirect taxes income. The leading sources of indirect taxes are sales tax and excise tax. The percentage of tax to the national income after the shutdown of the oil in 2012 is estimated not less than 40% (forty percent) of the national income.[225]

9.9. Major Tax Payers in South Sudan

Table 9.4: Shows major taxpayers in the Republic of South Sudan

No.	Individuals for personal income tax	Firms for business profit tax, sales tax and excise tax
1.	National Government employees	Construction Companies
2.	State Government employees	Petroleum Companies
3.	Local Government employees	Air lines Companies
4.	NGOs employees	Commercial Banks
5.	Companies employees	Forex Bureaus
6.	United Nations Organizations employees	Insurance Companies
7.	Central Bank employees	Manufacturing Companies
8.	Commercial Banks employees	Telecommunication Companies
9.		Hotels and Restaurants
10.		Bars

Source: Interview with Joseph Kenyi from the Revenue Department, Ministry of Finance, Juba.

---

225   Interview with Manyok Kuol Jok, Head of Taxation Office, Nimra Talata, Juba.

9.10. Sources of Revenue in the Republic of South Sudan
9.10.1. Sources of Revenue for the National Government in South Sudan

In according with Article 177 (2) of the Transitional Constitution of South Sudan, 2011, sources of revenue for the National Government of South Sudan are as follows:

a. petroleum, Gas/oil, mineral, and other natural resources;
b. national personal income tax;
c. corporate and business profit tax;
d. customs duties and import duties;
e. airports, rail, road, and river transport revenue;
f. service charges, fees and fines;
g. national government enterprises and projects;
h. value added tax or general sales tax on goods and services;
i. excise duties;
j. loans and borrowing from the Bank of South Sudan and the public;
k. grants-in-aid and foreign financial assistance;
l. fees from nationality, passports, immigration and visas; and
m. any other tax or revenue as may be determined by law.

9.10.2. Sources of Revenue of the States in South Sudan

In accordance with Article 179 of the Transitional Constitution of South Sudan, 2011, sources of revenue for the States of the Republic of South Sudan are as the following:

a. state land and property tax and royalties;
b. service charges for state services;
c. licenses issued by the state;
d. state personal income tax;
e. levies on tourism;
f. at least two percent of net oil and other mineral revenues for

each producing state;

g. state government projects;

h. stamp duties;

i. agricultural production taxes;

j. grants-in-aid and foreign aid;

k. excise duties;

l. other state taxes, which are not within the exclusive jurisdiction of the National Government;

m. loans and borrowing in accordance with Article 184 (2) and (3) of the Constitution; and

n. any other tax as may be determined by law.

9.10.3. Sources of Revenue for Local Government in the Republic of South Sudan

In accordance with Article 74 of the Local Government Act, 2009, of the Republic of South Sudan, sources of revenue for local government in South Sudan are categorized into: taxes, local rates and local earnings from investments and projects which are as follows:

a. **Taxes**

   i. council property tax;

   ii. social service tax;

   iii. council land tax;

   iv. animal tax;

   v. gibana tax;

   vi. council sales tax;

   vii. capital gains tax;

   viii. produce tax (ushur); and

   ix. any other taxes as may be authorized by law, rules and regulations.

b. **Local Rates**

   i.   user service charges;

   ii.   license fee;

  iii.   administrative fines;

  iv.   royalties;

   v.   permits;

  vi.   customary court fees and fines;

 vii.   contract fees;

viii.   any other fees and charges as may be authorized by any other law, rules and regulations.

c. **Local earnings from the council investments and projects.**

Local government institutions at times construct buildings inform of houses and shops or shelters in the markets. These structures are rented to whoever is in need to use those facilities. When those buildings are rented they become a source of revenue to the local councils whether in the rural or urban areas.

Chapter Ten

DEVELOPMENTS IN TAXATION

OF THE REPUBLIC OF SOUTH SUDAN

10.1. Amendment of Taxation Act, 2009

South Sudan Taxation Act, 2009, was amended in 2011, known as Taxation (Amendment Act, 2011). The purpose of Taxation Act, 2011, is to correct errors that were under Taxation Act, 2009, and to provide for related matters. The corrections made were as follows:

1. Section 64 of the Taxation Act, 2009, the words "*small or medium*" were deleted and replaced by "*Business organization*" which means any organization that is required to be registered pursuant to the provisions of this Act except an insurance company, an individual or organization of individuals liable for tax under Chapter XI of this Act.

2. Section 67: A business profit tax rate was set as in the table 10.1 below:

Table 10.1: Shows categories of business tax rate

N/S	Types of Business	Tax Rate
1.	Small Business/Enterprise	Ten percent (10%)
2.	Medium Business/Enterprise	Fifteen percent (15%)
3.	Large Business/Enterprise	Twenty percent (20%)

10.2. South Sudan Taxation Amendment Act, 2016

The South Sudan Taxation Amendment Act, 2016 was signed into law on 20th December 2016. The Act aims to increase government revenue by increasing various tax rates and introducing new categories of tax. The Act also aims to introduce proposal contained in the Finance Act, 2014/15 into the legislation.

10.3. Important Changes in South Sudan Taxation Amendment Act, 2016

1. The Act has introduced higher tax rates for withholding tax on rent, excise tax, sales tax and introduced new categories on income subject to withholding tax. It also seeks to widen the tax net by nullifying tax exemptions.
2. **Business Profit Tax:** With respect to business profit tax, the Act has nullified and avoided all tax exemptions which are not provided for in the Act. Provisions in the Investment Promotion Act have specifically been annulled by this new legislation.
3. **Advance Business Profit Tax on Imports:** Section 88 (a) of the Taxation Act has been removed. All unprocessed and

other food items considered to be basic necessity will now attract advance business profits tax at the rate of 2% while all other imported goods will attract a 4% tax.

4. The Minister of Finance has been designated as the sole authority to issue tax exemptions on imports.

5. **Personal Income Tax:** Personal income tax exemptions not provided in the Act, including those given to executive and legislative constitutional post holders, have been nullified. In addition, the amendment eliminates the possibility of voluntarily filing a personal income tax return where all tax has been withheld at service. The lowest personal income bracket has been changed, meaning that free personal income has been increased from SSP 300 to SSP 600.

6. **Withholding Tax:** A number of withholding tax measures have been introduced as follows:

   a. The South Sudan Government and Persons who pay technical fees to nonresidents have been appointed as withholding tax agents by paragraphs 92 (f), and (g) of the Act.

   b. The newly introduced rates of withholding tax on South Sudan Government contracts and payments of technical fees exceeding SSP 10,000 to nonresidents are 20% and 10% respectively.

   c. Section 92 has been amended by increasing the withholding on rent from 10% to 20%.

   d. Section 96, on tax payments deemed final and not subject to a credit or refunds, has been expanded to include the withholding tax on rents, contract payments, and technical fees paid to residents and nonresidents. Previously, only withholding tax on interest and dividends was deemed final payment tax.

7. **Sales Tax:** For sales tax purposes, the definition of hotel services has been expanded to include auxiliary services including but not limited to business centre services, massage service, swimming pool fees, and laundry services.

8. **Excise Tax:** The excise tax rate changes proposed in Finance Act 2014/15 have now been incorporated in the tax legislation. The new excise tax rates are as follows:

   a. Juices and soft drinks–10%.

   b. Beer and wine–50%.

   c. Spirits–25%.

   d. Tobacco products–100%.

   e. All transport and charters–20%.

   f. Motor cycles–50%.

9. **Tax Penalties:** The Act has introduced a grace period before the imposition of penalties for nonpayment of tax. Penalties will start accumulating on the first day of the fourth month after the month for which the tax payment was due.

10.4. Establishment of National Revenue Authority (NRA)

National Revenue Authority Act, 2016 was enacted in April 2016. The purpose of this Act is to provide for:

1. The establishment of an institution to be known as NRA.

2. To define duties, functions and responsibilities of the NRA.

3. Taking over the responsibilities and assets of the directorates of customs and taxation and non-tax collecting agencies.

4. The transfer of any other revenue collecting responsibilities of other governmental organizations to the NRA.

5. Any other matters related to the establishment of NRA.

National Revenue Authority is a body corporate with perpetual succession and a common seal. It is autonomous but under the supervision of the Minister of Finance and Planning and regularly reports to the National Legislative Assembly.

10.5. National Revenue Authority Vision

To be a topnotch revenue administration distinguished for providing unparalleled taxpayer service with professionalism, efficiency and integrity.

10.6. National Revenue Authority Mission

To mobilize non-oil revenue in a transparent, accountable, impartial, effective and efficient manner by providing unique quality taxpayer services that combine performance with values.

10.7. Authority of National Revenue Authority

NRA has authority to:

1. Assess, collect, remit and account for revenues due to the national government;
2. Administers and enforces laws pertaining to taxation in the country;
3. Promotes voluntary tax compliance by taxpayers as required by law or regulations;
4. Takes measures that counter-acts tax and customs fraud and any other forms of tax evasion;
5. Establishment and maintenance of electronic information management systems to increase efficiency, transparency and productivity of the revenue administration; and
6. Implementation of agreements and Memorandum of Understandings (MOUs) related to revenue administration pro-

grammes between GRSS, regional and international organizations and memoranda on matters related to imports/exports exemptions, trade facilitation and other related matters.

10.8. National Revenue Authority Board

NRA has an established Board of Directors comprising of nine directors as follows:

1. Chairman.
2. Five members, that is: Commissioner General, who shall be a non-voting member; one representative from the Ministry of Finance; one from the Ministry of Trade, Industry and Investment; one from the Ministry of Justice; and one from the Bank of South Sudan.
3. Three members from civil society institutions and private sector.

10.9. Responsibilities of the Board

The Board is responsible for:

1. Overseeing Authority including but not limited to approving organizational structures, general policies of the Authority including resources, services, property, personnel and contracts;
2. Provides oversight over the Commissioner General in connection with the implementation of the policies of the Authority.
3. Recommends to the Minister of Finance and Planning termination of service of the Commissioner General when he/she violate, misconduct or malpractices of the terms set in the code of conduct of the Authority; or inability, incapacity or incompetence to perform the duties of his/her office.

4. Approves the corporate business plan and the NRA's Strategic Plan.

10.10. National Revenue Authority Structure

NRA structure is comprised of five departments/commissions which are as below:

1. **Customs Commission**: Is responsible for collection of import duty, import sales tax, export duty, import excise and other taxes. The department also ensures the protection of revenue by preventing smuggling by physically patrolling the borders and other strategic points, examining goods and search premises as well as documents related to the goods. The department plays a key role in surmounting external aggression and maintains the territorial integrity of the department as part of the country's security network.

2. **Domestic Tax Revenue Commission**: Is charged with domestic tax administration covering registration of taxpayers, creating awareness to taxpayers, customer care services, and collection of direct and some indirect taxes pertaining to tax revenues and all non-tax revenues i.e. sales tax, income taxes, immigration and passports, traffic licenses, vehicles log books and work permits.

3. **Support Service Commission**: It merges the management of support services of finance, administration and research of the erstwhile agencies under this department. It will deal with specific affairs such as human resources, finance, logistics and ICT.

4. **Tax Audit and Compliance Commission**: It will deal with issues of monitoring the activities of compliance by the taxpayers in payment of the due taxes wholly, in time, and without corrupt practices by both the taxpayers and taxation officials.

5. **State Affairs Commission**: It will be responsible for the coordination of the country's states taxation affairs.

10.11. Revenue Collection

It has been very difficult from the budgetary records of the Ministry of Finance and Planning to find accurate figures of the revenue collected of all the units of government responsible for collection of revenue from 2011 up to 2017/18. The available records found are as in table 10.2 below:

Table 10.2: Shows revenue collected from August 2012 to May 2013

Month & Year	Collection (SSP)	Collection (USD)
August 2012	3,461,050.37	183,976.19
September 2012	6,873,146.01	105,396.28
October 2012	11,174,009.10	121,107.81
November 2012	9,359,069.46	
December 2012	9,023,710.71	
January 2013	12,662,744.04	
February 2013	9,290,307.79	
March 2013	13,080,184.93	
April 2013	14,909,216.40	
May 2013	18,617,130.09	
Total	**108,450,568.90**	**410,480.28**

Source: Interview with Late John Joseph Ucin, Assistant Director for Large Taxpayers Unit, Taxation Office, Nimra Talata, Juba.

However, it was the revenue collected at the time when the NRA started to supervise the collection is when regular record of accurate figures emerged. The collection of revenue under the supervision of NRA started from 1st January 2019. The figures in table 10.3 below shows the amounts collected from 1st January to 15th August 2019 and were remitted to the Block Account of the Ministry of Finance and Planning. The remittances exclude the banks' collection charges and 2% for NRA establishment fund.

Table 10.3: Shows revenue collected from 1st January to 15th August 2019

S/No.	Month	Collection SSP	Collection USD	Amount Remitted USD	Amount Remitted SSP
1	January	1,288,719,019.00	4,733,884.08	4,601,335.33	1,252,634,886.47
2	February	1,113,687,237.15	9,198,933.98	8,941,363.83	1,082,503,994.51
3	March	1,155,212,936.01	5,686,380.11	5,527,161.47	1,122,866,973.80
4	April	1,541,209,198.88	5,572,443.40	5,416,414.98	1,498,055,341.31
5	May	1,162,487,925.00	7,830,932.34	7,709680.62	1,129,938,262.90
6	June	1,123,569,977.01	3,884,776.11	3,873,202.75	1,091,837,004.40
7	July	1,514,141,272.44	5,045,839.23	4,904,555.73	1,471,745,316.81
8	August 1-15	745,844,873.52	2,363,341.52	2,297,167.96	724,961,217.06
TO-TAL		9,644,872,439.01	$44,316,530.77	$43,270,882.67	9,374,542,997.26

Source: NRA Establishment Progress Report from May 2018 to August 2019.

References

Akrani, Gaurav. "Meaning of Public Expenditure". Retrieved 15 February 2012.

Amadeo, Kimberly. "Government Subsidies (Farm, Oil, Export, etc.)". The Balance. Retrieved 03/16/2018.

Bhatia, H.L. Public Finance. 26th Edition, Vikas Publishing House PVT Ltd., 2008.

British Museum. "History of the World in 100 Objects: Rosetta Stone." BBC.

Cambridge, UK: Cambridge Judge Business School, University of Cambridge. Retrieved 2016-06-27."Measuring fossil fuel 'hidden' costs". University of Cambridge Judge Business School. 23 July 2015. Retrieved 2016-06-27.

Cambridge, UK: Cambridge Judge Business School, University of Cambridge. Retrieved 2016-06-27.

"Chapter 3: Subsidy types". Global Subsidies Initiative IISD. Archived from the original *on 2012-09-05*.Retrieved 2015-05-03.

Cohen, R. (2008). "Playing by the NFL's Tax Exempt Rulesh". *Non Profit Quarterly*. Retrieved 2013-04-15.

Collins Dictionary of Economics. Is That a Good State/Local Economic Development Deal? Retrieved 2013-09-05.

"Darius I (Darius the Great), King of Persia (from 521 BC)". 1902 encyclopedia.com.net.Retrieved 22 January 2013.

David F. Burg (2004). A World History of Tax Rebellions, Taylor and Francis.

Durban, South Africa: Vth World Parks Congress: Sustainable Finance Stream. Archived from the original (PDF) on *2013-12-03*.How Farm Subsidies Harm Taxpayers, Consumers, and Farmers, Too. Who Benefits from Farm Subsidies?

Food and Agriculture Organization. Retrieved 03/16/2018.

Fowler, P.; Fokker, R. (2004). A Sweeter Future? The potential for EU sugar reform to contribute to poverty reduction in Southern Africa. Oxford: Oxfam International. ISBN 9781848141940.

"FT Lexicon" *The Financial Times.*

Geoffrey Morse & David Williams. Davies: Principles of Tax Law. Fifth Edition, Sweet and Maxwell Ltd. London, England, 2004.

Government of Southern Sudan Approved Budget 2011. Ministry of Finance and Planning: Approved by Southern Sudan Legislative Assembly on 14th March 2011. [GoSS Revenues and Expenditures: 2005-2011].

Government of Southern Sudan. The Taxation Act, 2009.

. "History of Iran (Persia)." Historyworld.net. Retrieved 22 January 2013.

Hoffman, Phillipe and Kathryn Norberg (1994), Fiscal Crises, Liberty, and Representatives. Retrieved 21 January 2013.

Hope, Chris; Gilding, Paul; Alvarez, Jimena (2015). Quantifying the implicit climate subsidy received by leading fossil fuel companies—Working Paper No. 02/2015 (PDF).

Indra Overland (2010) 'Subsidies for Fossil Fuels and Climate Change: A Comparative Perspective', *International Journal of Environmental Studies,* Vol. 67, No. 3.

Is That a Good State/Local Economic Development Deal? A Checklist (2014-06-03), Naked Capitalism.

Kolb, R.W. (2008). "Subsidies". Encyclopedia of business ethics and society. Thousand Oaks: Sage Publications. *ISBN 9781412916523.*

Laws of South Sudan. Appropriation Act, 2017/18, September, 2017.

Laws of South Sudan. Financial Act, 2017, September, 2017. P. 11

Laws of Southern Sudan. The Local Government Act, 2009.

Laws of the Republic of South Sudan. The Transitional Constitution of the Republic of South Sudan, 2011.

Manas'she, P.N. A Textbook of Business Finance. McMore Accounting Books, Nairobi, 1990.

Mick Moore, Wilson Prichard and Odd-Helge F. Jeldstad. Taxing Africa: Coercion, Reform and Development, Zed Books Ltd., London, UK, 2018.

Morse, G. and Williams, D. Davies: Principles of Tax Law. Fifth Edition, Sweet & Maxwell Ltd., 2004.

Mutamba, A.H. MK Fundamental Economics. East Africa Edition. MK Publishers LTD., Kampala, Uganda, 2009.

Myers, N. (1996). "Perverse Subsidies" (PDF). *Sixth Ordinary Meeting of the Conference of the Parties to the Convention on Biological Diversity.*

Myers, N. (1997). "Perverse subsidies". In Costanza, R.; Norgaard, R.; Daly, H.; Goodland, R.; Cumberland, J. An Introduction to Ecological Economics. Boca Raton, Fla.: St. Lucie Press. ISBN 1884015727.

Myers, N. (1998). "Lifting the veil on perverse subsidies".

Myers, N.; Kent, J. (2001). Perverse subsidies: how tax dollars can undercut the environment and the economy. Washington, DC: Island Press. *ISBN 1-55963-835*

Myers, N. (2008). "Perverse Priorities" (PDF). IUCN Opinion Piece.

OECD (2003). "Perverse incentives in biodiversity loss" (PDF). Working Party on Global and Structural Policies Working Group on Economic Aspects of Biodiversity.

"OECD Revenue Statistics: 1965-2016".

Oxford English Dictionary *(3rd ed.). Oxford University Press. September 2005.*

Porter, G. (1998). "Natural Resource Subsidies, Trade and Environment: The Cases of Forest and Fisheries" (PDF). Center for Environmental Law.

Portugal, L. (2002). "OECD Work on Defining and Measuring Subsidies in Agriculture". The OECD Workshop on Environmentally Harmful Subsidies, Paris, 7–8 November 2002.

"Report of the Expert Consultation on Identifying, Assessing and Reporting on Subsidies in the Fishing Industry - Rome, 3-6 December 2002".

Republic of South Sudan, Laws of South Sudan. National Revenue Authority Act, 2016.

Republic of South Sudan, Ministry of Finance and Economic Planning. Approved Budget, Financial Year 2014/15 (August 2014).

Republic of South Sudan. The Approved National Budget Plan and the Approved Budget 2013/14. Ministry of Finance, Commerce, Investment and Economic Planning.

Republic of South Sudan, National Development Strategy.

Consolidate Peace and Stabilize the Economy, July 2018-June 2021.

Robin, S.; Wolcott, R.; Quintela, C.E. (2003). Perverse Subsidies and the Implications for Biodiversity: A review of recent findings and the status of policy reforms (PDF).

Saleemi, N.A. Taxation I Simplified (Revised Edition), Saleemi Publications Ltd., Nairobi, Kenya, 2007.

Santandrea, P. Stefano. A Tribal History of the Western Bahr El Ghazal. Italy, 1964.

Steenblik, R. (1998). "Previous Multilateral Efforts to Discipline Subsidies to Natural Resource Based Industries" (PDF).

Sudan People's Liberation Movement, National Secretariat. Secretariat of Planning & Economic Affairs, SPLM National Economic Taskforce (SPLM/NET). Brainstorming on NilePet Fuel Price Subsidy, October 23, 2017.

Superior Court of Pennsylvania *(1894)*. "Brooke et al versus the City of Philadelphia et al". Weekly Notes of Cases Argued and Determined in the Supreme Court of Pennsylvania, the County Courts of Philadelphia, and the United States District and Circuit Courts for the Eastern District of Pennsylvania. Kay and brother.

The Taxation Chamber. Taxation Guide, Khartoum University Press, Khartoum, Sudan, November, 2003.

Taxes in the Ancient World, *University of Pennsylvania Almanac*, Vol. 48, No. 28, 2 April, 2002.

Theobald, A. B. The Mahdiya: A History of the Anglo-Egyptian, 1881-1899. Longmans, Green and Co. Ltd., London, Great Britain, 1962.

The Republic of South Sudan. The Approved Budget Fiscal Year 2015/16. Ministry of Finance and Economic Planning October 2015.

The Republic of South Sudan, Ministry of Finance and Planning. Approved National Budget Plan and Approved Budget for FY 2016/17. December 2016.

United States Department of the Treasury."Bureau of the Public Debt Homepage". Retrieved October 12, 2010.

United States Department of the Treasury. "FAQs: National Debt". Archived from the original on October 21, 2010. Retrieved October 12, 2010.

William J. McCluskey; Riël C. D. Franzsen (2005). Land value Taxation; An Applied Analysis.

Workshop on the Impact of Government Financial Transfers on Fisheries Management, Resource Sustainability, and International Trade. Retrieved 2013-08-05.

Index